PUBLISHED FOR THE MALONE SOCIETY BY
OXFORD UNIVERSITY PRESS

GREAT CLARENDON STREET, OXFORD OX2 6DP

Oxford New York
Athens Auckland Bangkok Bogota Bombay Buenos Aires
Calcutta Cape Town Dar es Salaam Delhi Florence Hong Kong Istanbul
Karachi Kuala Lumpur Madras Madrid Melbourne Mexico City
Nairobi Paris Singapore Taipei Tokyo Toronto Warsaw

and associated companies in
Berlin Ibadan

ISBN 0 19 729035 3

Printed by BAS Printers Limited, Over Wallop, Hampshire

THE SHEPHERDS' PARADISE
BY
WALTER MONTAGU

THE MALONE SOCIETY
REPRINTS, VOL. 159
1997

This edition of *The Shepherds' Paradise* was prepared by Sarah Poynting and checked by the General Editor.

The Society is grateful to the Folger Shakespeare Library for permission to edit the text of its manuscript Vb 203, and to reproduce four pages.

December 1997 ROGER HOLDSWORTH

LIST OF SIGLA

FTix	Folger Library manuscript Vb 203
FCos	Folger Library manuscript Vb 204
BSt	British Library manuscript Stowe 976
BSl	British Library manuscript Sloane 3649
BPet	British Library Additional manuscript 41617
8°	The printed edition of 1659

The sigla of manuscripts refer to the earliest provenance currently known.

INTRODUCTION

WALTER MONTAGU wrote *The Shepherds' Paradise*, probably in 1632, to be performed by Queen Henrietta Maria and the ladies of her court. There are five surviving manuscript copies of the play, three in the British Library (Stowe 976, Sloane 3649, and Additional manuscript 41617) and two in the Folger Shakespeare Library, Washington (Vb 203 and Vb 204, described by Bentley as manuscripts 4662 and 4661 respectively[1]). It is likely that a sixth copy, or part of a copy, was still extant in the nineteenth century, since Hazlitt's *Manual of Plays* includes the entry 'Bellessa, the Shepherd's Queen: the Scene, Galicia. An unpublished and incomplete drama in prose and verse. Fol.'.[2] This cannot refer to any of the five known manuscripts, as only BSt, which has a few leaves missing at the end of Act IV, could be regarded as in any way incomplete, and this text does not contain the opening description of the scene as being set in Galicia.

The play was entered in the Stationers' Company Register on 27 September 1658 by Thomas Dring, and published by him in an octavo edition the following year. A variant imprint gives the publisher as John Starkey.

The present edition is a near-diplomatic transcription of Folger Vb 203, the Tixall manuscript.

THE OCCASION

Walter Montagu (?1603–77), the second son of the Earl of Manchester, was not a natural choice for this high-profile theatrical undertaking, for his previous activities as a protégé of the Duke of Buckingham had been in the fields of espionage and diplomacy rather than literature or drama. Following the Duke's murder in 1628 he found a new, and for the time being rather less dangerous, protector in the person of Henrietta Maria, whom he had first met in 1624–5 during the negotiations for her marriage with Charles. He established himself as a central member of her court at Denmark (Somerset) House, where he was remembered as having 'enjoyed the pleasures of the World in a very great Measure and Excess'.[3] French envoys commented with some concern on the closeness of his relationship with the Queen, St. Chamond reporting that Montagu showed evidence of 'une grande passion au service de la Royne, elle ayme son esprit et sa conversation, toutes fois sans aucun scandale'.[4] But the scandal which did occur was not sexual but political. Montagu, Henry Jermyn, and Henry Percy, led by the Earl of Holland, involved the Queen in an Anglo-French conspiracy to unseat the Lord Treasurer, the Earl of Portland, in England, and Cardinal Richelieu in France, as a first step, in the minds of at least some members of the faction, towards unseating Louis XIII himself and replacing him with Gaston

[1] G. E. Bentley, *The Jacobean and Caroline Stage*, 7 vols. (Oxford, 1941–68), iv. 917.

[2] William Carew Hazlitt (ed.), *A Manual for the Collector and Amateur of Old English Plays* (London, 1892), p. 25.

[3] Edward Hyde, *The Life of the Earl of Clarendon* (1759), p. 120.

[4] St. Chamond to Richelieu, 15 June 1632, PRO 31/3/67.

d'Orléans. The intrigue came to a head in 1632 and 1633, and it was in this context that *The Shepherds' Paradise* was written and performed.

It is possible that Montagu did not write his play without some assistance. In particular, the style of the Prologue, some of the revision of FTix, and, less clearly, the songs between the acts, suggest a different hand. Aurelian Townshend has been proposed as a collaborator,[5] but a more likely candidate is Thomas Killigrew. Killigrew was not yet a dramatist in his own right, but he was a companion of Montagu's, and lover (later husband) of the maid of honour Cicely Crofts, who played the part of Agenor. Moreover, he reused both character-names and only slightly revised dialogue from *The Shepherds' Paradise* in his *Bellamira* (written *c.*1650), and drew attention to their provenance by references to 'the most excellent *Bellessa*' and 'divine *Bellessa*'.[6] Killigrew's frequent practice of 'borrowing', especially from earlier plays, may be responsible for the occasional echoes of other works that can be heard in *The Shepherds' Paradise*.[7]

Henrietta Maria, 'some of her ladies, and all her maides of honour' began rehearsing the play 'wherein her Ma^ty^ is pleased to act a parte, as well for her recreation as for the exercise of her Englishe'[8] in September 1632, intending to present it to the King at Denmark House for his birthday on 19 November. The earliest recorded critical response to the play came in November, John Pory writing to Viscount Scudamore that:

> On Wedensday night his Majesty among other lordes meeting with my lord Privy Seale at St Jameses, did highly congratulate and extoll unto him the rare and excellent partes of his sonne Mr. Walter Montague, appearing in the Pastorall which hee hath penned for her Majesty her Ladies, and maydes to acte upon his Majesties birthday. And it seems his Majesty was in good earnest: for hee hath given him for that service £2000 out of the Queens portion-money, and her Majesty hath given him £500 out of her owne purse. Mr Taylour the Player hath also the making of a knight given him for teaching them how to act the Pastorall.[9]

[5] Louis Martz, *The Wit of Love* (Notre Dame, Ind., 1969), pp. 87–8.

[6] Thomas Killigrew, *Comedies and Tragedies* (1663), sigs. Nnn4^v^ and Qqq2^r^. Killigrew appears to have been working from memory rather than a copy of the manuscript: when Arcus the Moor says that 'what is not like me is beautiful . . . the curse of an incens'd deity lives in our black', Bellamira replies '. . . I rather think, like divine *Bellessa*, beauty, afraid of injuries, or in revenge of that inconstancy she has found in men, hath thrown off red and white; and to live safe from the vanity and perjury of both sexes hath made this retreat into black for her security' (sig. Qqq2^r^). The sentiment attributed to Bellessa is clearly adapted from a speech by Genorio (cf. FTix, 1524–7), and it seems likely that Killigrew confused it with Bellessa's reproof to Moramante when he votes against Gemella's admission to the Society (in BSl and FTix (1772–86) only). It is also possible that Killigrew's involvement was in hearing the lines of the cast, or acting as bookholder, rather than as co-author.

[7] Compare, for example, Bellessa's curse (3336–7) with *Romeo and Juliet* II. ii. 161–2, and the closing verse (3853–4) with Jonson's 'To the Most Noble, and above his Titles, Robert, Earl of Somerset' (ll. 23–4).

[8] John Pory to Sir Thomas Puckering, 20 September 1632, British Library Harleian MS 7000, Fol. 336.

[9] 3 November 1632, PRO C115/M35/8416. Printed in microfiche appendix to William S. Powell, *John Pory 1572–1636: The Life and Letters of a Man of Many Parts* (Chapel Hill, NC, 1977).

The gossip concerning Joseph Taylor's knighthood proved unfounded, and it is probable that the payment to Montagu was similarly non-existent, but these rumours are at least suggestive of the significance attached not only to the occasion, but to the play, particularly in the light of Charles's more usual hostility to Montagu.

Complaints concerning the length of *The Shepherds' Paradise* emerged from the rehearsals, Pory reporting that 'my lady Marques her part a lone is as long as an ordinary playe', and it may have been at this point that it was realized that a shorter version of the play was needed.[10] Its length evidently caused problems for the actresses: the Tuscan resident Salvetti noted on 9 November 1632 that 'Her Majesty the queen rehearses her pastoral every day. Nevertheless she will not be able to perform it on the 29th [i.e. 19th], the king's birthday, because none of the ladies performing in it with her are ready, neither is the apparatus for the scenery', and on 23 November he reported again that 'they have not yet announced the day for the queen's pastoral, because the performers are not all ready'.[11]

The performers who were finding the play so difficult—presumably they were expected to learn their lines—included twelve women of the Queen's court, as well as Henrietta Maria herself, who played the lead role of Bellessa. The cast consisted of her six maids of honour, Cicely Crofts (Agenor),[12] Sophia Carew (Fidamira),[13] Goditha Arden (the King of Castile),[14] Ellenor Villiers (Pantamora),[15] Elizabeth Howard (Melidoro),[16] and Dorothy Seymour (Osorio and Romero);[17] the Mother of the Maids, Ursula Beaumont (Votorio),[18] whose daughter Elizabeth may have been the M[rs] Beaumont who played the small part of Bonorio; and four court ladies, Anne Kirke (Camena),[19] the twelve-year-old Victoria Cary (Martiro),[20] Lady

[10] Pory to Scudamore, 27 October 1632, PRO C115/M35/8424, in Powell's appendix.

[11] Quoted from the translation in John Orrell, 'Amerigo Salvetti and the London Court Theatre, 1616–1640', *Theatre Survey*, 20 (1979), 17–18 (a transcript of Salvetti's comments on the theatre taken from British Library Add. MS 27962).

[12] (?–1638); daughter of Sir John Crofts of Saxham; m. Thomas Killigrew, 1636.

[13] (?–1703); daughter of Sir George Carew and Thomasina Godolphin; m. (1) Richard Neville, son of Sir Christopher Neville; (2) Walter Stewart, third son of the 1st Lord Blantyre. One of her daughters was Frances Teresa ('La Belle') Stuart.

[14] Daughter of Sir Henry Arden of Park Hall, Warwickshire (an old Roman Catholic family), and Dorothy Feilding; m. (Sir) Herbert Price; was still alive when he died in 1678.

[15] (?–1685); daughter of Sir Edward Villiers and Barbara St. John; had an illegitimate son by Henry Jermyn in December/January 1632–3.

[16] Probably the daughter of Sir Charles Howard, fourth son of the Earl of Suffolk, and Mary Fitz.

[17] Daughter of Sir Edward Seymour of Bury Pomeroy, Devon, and Dorothy Killigrew. Alive in 1663, when she was still described as maid of honour to Henrietta Maria, then the Queen Mother.

[18] (?–1635); possibly the widow of Sir Francis Beaumont the dramatist.

[19] 1607–41; daughter of Sir Robert Killigrew, the Queen's Vice-Chamberlain, and Mary Woodhouse; m. George Kirke, Gentleman of the Robes to Charles I; drowned July 1641 when the Queen's barge overturned coming under London Bridge.

[20] (1620–94); daughter of Sir Henry Cary, 1st Viscount Falkland and Elizabeth Tanfield; m. (1) Sir William Uvedale (after the death of his son, to whom she had been engaged); (2) Bartholomew Price.

Anne Feilding (Timante),[21] and the Marchioness of Hamilton,[22] who played opposite the Queen as the male lead, Basilino, cast, perhaps, on the basis of her rank. Of these, only the last three and Sophia Carew (after 1633 under her married name of Neville) ever performed in court masques, and it is worth noting that none of the 'great ladies' from the court's old aristocratic families took part in the play.

That the scenery, like the actresses, was not ready is hardly surprising, as it was not until 3 November that a warrant was issued to Inigo Jones authorizing him to have a 'roome' constructed at Denmark House for the presentation of the play.[23] As the accounts of the Office of Works show, the 'roome' consisted of a temporary new masquing house built of pine in the paved lower court, which was roofed over and the open sides walled in, at a total cost of £341. 16*s.* 11*d.*, including a charge for altering the house for a masque and dismantling it when both productions were finished.[24] John Orrell, in articles drawing on these accounts, as well as on the diary of Jones's assistant John Webb, has convincingly identified a previously unidentified drawing in the British Library[25] as being the plan of this temporary structure, which was briefly described by the French ambassador, the Marquis de Fontenay-Mareuil, in a letter reporting on the 'préparatifs magnifiques' being made by the Queen for the production: 'qu'elle doit représenter dans la seconde Cour de Somerset, où l'on a eslevé un Couvert Dais de sapin de la grandeur de la Cour mesme pour separer du mauvois'.[26] The interior of the room, which measured 75 feet by 34 feet, with wider 'outlets' or extensions at the stage end, where the total width was 51 feet 6 inches, was fitted with 'degrees' (seating tiers) on three sides, a low stage with five shallow steps at the centre front, and 'diverse ingines and motions' for scenery. The stage right extension served as a 'musickhouse'. The building was 25 feet high, allowing access from the Upper Court to the highest of the degrees at the back of the auditorium. The room was only two-fifths of the size of the masquing house built five years later at Whitehall, and alterations were made to it following the play in order to increase the floor space for dancing.

[21] Either the wife (born Anne Weston, daughter of the Lord Treasurer) or the sister of Basil Lord Feilding. Both married during Christmas 1632, so that correct identification depends on the date of the Stowe manuscript, in which the cast list first appears. The sister, who married Baptist Noel, Viscount Campden, is the more likely candidate.

[22] (1613–38); daughter of William Feilding, Earl of Denbigh, and Susan Villiers, sister of the Duke of Buckingham; m. at the age of seven to James Hamilton, 3rd Marquis, later 1st Duke of Hamilton.

[23] 'The Lord Chamberlain's Dramatic Records', *Collections Volume II*, Malone Society (Oxford, 1931), p. 359.

[24] 'Dramatic Records in the Declared Accounts of the Office of Works', *Collections Volume X*, Malone Society (Oxford, 1977), pp. 44–5.

[25] British Library Lansdowne MS 1171, Fols. 9b–10a.

[26] John Orrell, 'The Paved Court Theatre at Somerset House', *British Library Journal*, 3 (1977), 13–19; *The Theatres of Inigo Jones and John Webb* (Cambridge, 1985), pp. 113–27; Fontenay-Mareuil to Bouthillier (French Secretary of State), 26 November 1632, PRO 31/3/67: 'which she is to perform in the second courtyard at Somerset House, where they have raised a pine canopy covering the whole extent of the courtyard to keep out the bad weather'.

The raked stage was 25 feet 4 inches deep, and the width at the proscenium 34 feet, but much of this space was taken up by scenery, and the acting area cannot have been more than twelve feet in depth and between thirty feet downstage and rather less than ten feet upstage in width. Orrell suggests that the main acting area was the level space in front of the stage, which measured 34 feet by eight feet, though it seems more likely that this constituted a secondary acting area, as the perspective scenery would only have been fully effective if the primary area had been the stage itself. In addition to the backcloth, the plan shows grooves for back shutters, four pairs of flat wings, and the proscenium and standing scene; between the back shutters and the backcloth are three pairs of posts to support relieve scenes.[27] Orgel and Strong estimate from the design drawings that 'there were at least eight changes of scene, and probably several more'.[28]

Of particular interest among the designs is a rough sketch on the verso of a shutter design for the first scene ('a pallas in trees'), which shows

> a sketch of masquers revealed in tableau: ten figures sitting in two tiers within a grotto with two figures flying above them. At the top there is a fragmentary inscription: *The first* [. . .] [. . .] /91 [. . .]/*Pallas as painted with the* [. . .] *standing sceane*.

Orgel and Strong comment that 'There is no apparent connection between this and the contents of the play, although the fragmentary inscription . . . should relate to *The Shepherd's Paradise*.'[29] The connection with the play becomes clear from looking at the Sloane and Tixall manuscripts, which are alone in containing the prologue printed in the present edition: the two flying figures are evidently Apollo and Diana, while each of the ten seated figures plays a God who has 'put himselfe into a starre' (line 14), and who presumably carried a candle to light the stage. There is no evidence as to the identities or sex of these masquers, nor as to whether the prologue was spoken or, as is possible, sung, but the drawing, as well as providing information about the masque-like staging of the opening of the play, serves to confirm that this was the version of the text used in performance.[30]

A few of the costume designs have also survived. These are elegant and graceful adaptations of contemporary fashion, with the exception of the design for one of Fidamira's costumes, which is more formal and old-fashioned, and which Orgel and Strong have shown to be based on a Spanish

[27] See Richard Southern, *Changeable Scenery* (London, 1952), *passim* (but especially pp. 60–74) for a discussion of the operation of the scenery.

[28] Stephen Orgel and Roy Strong, *Inigo Jones: Theatre of the Stuart Court*, 2 vols. (London, 1973), ii. 506. The surviving set designs are reproduced on pp. 504–21 of the same volume. Orrell, *The Theatres of Inigo Jones and John Webb*, p. 204, n. 19, further suggests that Orgel and Strong's drawing 136, tentatively assigned by them to the 1626 production of *Artenice* (i. 388) actually belongs to *The Shepherds' Paradise*.

[29] Orgel and Strong, *Inigo Jones*, ii. 507.

[30] It also tends to confirm Louis Martz's argument in *The Wit of Love*, pp. 80–9, that Thomas Carew's problematic lines 54–88 in his poem 'In answer of an Elegiacall Letter upon the death of the King of Sweden from Aurelian Townshend . . .' refer to Montagu's play, not to Townshend's *Tempe Restored*.

portrait of a Hapsburg Infanta.[31] The male costumes are of interest in revealing how Jones dealt with the problem of cross-dressing, which had caused offence when the Queen and her French ladies took part in *Artenice* in 1626: the designs for Basilino and his father the King of Castile put the actresses in short, loose dresses coming to just below the knee. Masculinity was suggested, particularly in accessories such as hats and footwear, and in the carrying of swords or canes, rather than imitated literally. A comparison of the two sketches for the King's costume shows how it was softened and feminized during the design process.[32]

The Shepherds' Paradise was finally ready for performance at the beginning of 1633, after a last delay caused by a brief period of mourning for the Elector Palatine, and was produced on 9 January to a rather thin audience, Sir Robert Phelips's newswriter telling him that 'the difficulty of getting in on Wednesday being such or so apprehended, that there was a scarcitie of spectators'.[33] In view of this, he reported, a second performance was planned for Candlemas Day, 2 February, in order to allow those who had missed the first performance to see the play. There is no specific report of its having taken place, but the Revels Accounts for 3 February show a charge for '5 mens worke day and night at a dancing & play' 'for the Queenes Ma:tie at Denmarke house'.[34] It is likely that the temporary playhouse was then adapted for an unknown masque performed on Shrove Tuesday, 5 March. Both Bentley and Orgel and Strong suggest that the production recorded as having taken place on 5 March was another performance of *The Shepherds' Paradise*, but John Orrell's arguments, drawing on records not used by the earlier writers, in favour of a masque carry greater conviction.[35]

Reception

The day after the January performance Beaulieu wrote to Puckering that the 'costly pastoral' had lasted seven or eight hours.[36] Unfortunately he was not actually present, so we cannot be sure of the accuracy of the report, or, if it was true, whether the time was entirely taken up by the performance of the text, or whether it included dancing, as seems possible, or even breaks for

[31] The costume designs are reproduced in Orgel and Strong, *Inigo Jones*, ii. 522–35; the Spanish portrait is discussed on p. 522 and printed on p. 529.

[32] Drawings 264 and 265 in Orgel and Strong, *Inigo Jones*, ii. 532, 534.

[33] *Hombre fiel* to Sir Robert Phelips, 13 January [1633], Historical Manuscripts Commission, Third Report, Appendix, p. 282; also printed in Bentley, *The Jacobean and Caroline Stage*, iv. 918.

[34] *Collections Volume XIII*, Malone Society (Oxford, 1986), pp. 121–2.

[35] Bentley, *The Jacobean and Caroline Stage*, vi. 86; Orgel and Strong *Inigo Jones*, ii. 505; John Orrell, 'Productions at the Paved Court Theatre, Somerset House, 1632–3', *Notes and Queries*, 221 (1976), 223–5.

[36] Thomas Birch (ed.), *Court and Times of Charles I*, 2 vols. (London, 1848), ii. 216.

eating, such as Salvetti recorded during the following year's production of *The Faithful Shepherdess*.[37] We cannot, therefore, infer from Beaulieu's statement that it was the uncut version of the text that was acted, but in attempting to assess the play's reception, critics (having available only the 1659 edition) have dwelt with understandable sympathy on jokes about its length and incomprehensibility, while disregarding evidence of more favourable responses. Suckling's mockery in 'The Wits (A Sessions of the Poets)', in which Apollo, in a trial to decide who should be awarded the laureateship, demands of Montagu,

> If he understood his own Pastoral.
> For
> If he could do it, 'twould plainly appear
> He understood more than any man there,
> And did merit the Bayes above all the rest,
> But the Mounsier was modest, and silence confest.[38]

has led Stephen Orgel, for example, to write that 'The play was found tedious and its message obscure'.[39]

However, two letters from Lucius Cary, Viscount Falkland, the first asking to borrow a manuscript of the play, and the second written on the return of the part of the manuscript he was lent, provide us with a contrary view.[40] His praise of the play in the first letter may simply be conventional compliment:

> I must say this, both of it and the great actresse of it, that her action was worthy of it, and it was worthy of her action, and I beleeue the world can fitt nether of them, but with one another.

[37] Orrell, 'Amerigo Salvetti', p. 19.

[38] Sir John Suckling, *The Non-Dramatic Works*, ed. Thomas Clayton (Oxford, 1971), pp. 74–5. Patrick Cary was similarly derisive in his poem 'And can You thincke that this Translation': 'But tell mee pray, if ever you | Read th'*English* of *Watt Mountague*, | Is't not more hard then *French*?' (*Poems*, ed. Sister Veronica Delany (Oxford, 1978), p. 16.) Cary was still a child in 1633, and it seems quite probable, as Elsie Duncan-Jones suggests, that the play was a family joke, especially since his sister Victoria played Martiro, the deliberately obscure poet of impossibility (*Notes and Queries*, 200 (1955), 404–7). It could be, though, that the poem, written in 1650–1, refers to Montagu's recently published first volume of *Miscellanea Spiritualia* (1648).

[39] Orgel and Strong, *Inigo Jones*, i. 63.

[40] PRO MS SP/534/112. The two letters contained in this manuscript, which are copies lacking details of date and recipient, have been misdated as written in 1634 in the *Calendar of State Papers (Domestic)* on the basis of a reference to the recent widowhood of Lady Dorothy Shirley, whose husband actually died on 8 February 1633. The correction in the dating, together with the internal evidence of the contents, make it almost certain that the letters concern *The Shepherds' Paradise*.

but in his second letter Falkland is very pressing in his request to read the rest of the play (implying a longer text than that of any masque),[41] and to take a copy of it for himself:

I haue here returned, what I had much rather haue kept, but that I am enioyned to restitucon, & my comfort is y^{t} the parteing with this, will purchase me the readeing of the rest, if I valued it so high at the single hearing, when myne eares could not catch halfe the words, what must I do now, in the reading when I may pause vppon it. but what should I doe if I might enioy a Coppy of it, or haue leaue to Coppy it, wch fauo^{r} I hope I shall one day obtaine, for it is not twice or thrise reading this peece, that will sufficiently satisfie a well advised reader . . .

Even these generous comments suggest that the audience found the play inherently undramatic, a piece that requires to be read more than 'twice or thrise' if its meaning is to be grasped. Falkland's comment about not being able to 'catch halfe the words' suggests, though, that the incomprehensibility of the play may have been a result not so much of Montagu's prose as of poor acoustics, inexperienced acting, and the Queen's French accent.

The only certain report from a member of the audience, that by Salvetti, diplomatically lays emphasis on the beauty of the scenery and the excellence of the Queen's performance, without mentioning the play:

. . . the scenic apparatus was very lovely, but so was the beauty of the performers, and of the queen above all the rest, who with her English and the grace with which she showed it off, together with her regal gestures . . . outdid all the other ladies though they too acted their parts with the greatest variety.[42]

Praise of Henrietta Maria's performance was evidently *de rigueur*: '[she] is said to have really excelled all others both in acting and singing';[43] Carew's description of 'The Beauties of the SHEPHERDS PARADISE' in his verse letter to Townshend culminates in a eulogy on her singing, and Townshend's 'On Hearing Her Majesty Sing' may also have been written in tribute to her

[41] It is possible that what he borrowed were the first two acts of FCos, a text written by four scribes in separate sections, of which Acts I and II make up the first, or the lost incomplete copy described by Hazlitt, which, from the spelling of 'Bellessa' and the description of the scene as 'Galicia', is likely to have been most closely related to FCos. Falkland's letters provide valuable information about the circulation and use of the manuscripts: he also writes in the first letter of reading the play 'to a ffreind or two, that are Iudges, (if it be possible) fitt for it', and in the second that 'one of ye fayrest, wittiest and newest widdowes of o^{r} time, Lady Dorothy Sherly, longs extreamely to read it, and hath sent to beg a sight of it'.

[42] Orrell 'Amerigo Salvetti', p. 18.

[43] *Hombre fiel* to Sir Robert Phelips, 13 January 1633; Bentley, *The Jacobean and Caroline Stage*, iv. 918. It is significant that there appears to have been no criticism of the enterprise in circles surrounding the court similar to that made of the 1626 performance by the Queen and her French ladies. In part this may have been because of a change in court culture which made the women's acting more acceptable, as is suggested by the lack of severe restrictions on entry to the audience like those enforced in 1626, but it may also reflect a degree of prudence in view of the furore which arose very soon after the January production over Prynne's *Histriomastix* and its attack on 'Women Actors: Notorious Whores'.

on this occasion, in response to Carew's urging him to turn his talents to praising 'These harmelesse pastimes'.[44]

The popularity of the song performed as a solo by Henrietta Maria in Act V of *The Shepherds' Paradise* (see ll. 2886–3003) is confirmed by the fact that it appears to have been circulated in manuscript separately from the play, though the evidence is ambiguous. A commonplace book in the Bodleian Library contains a comic poem in praise of gambling, 'Lord Goring's Verses', rather unimaginatively constructed from lines of love poems by Donne, Suckling, Wither, and Davenant.[45] The opening couplet is taken from the first two lines of Montagu's song, 'Presse me noe more kind love, I will confesse | And tell you all, nay rather more then lesse' (2986–7), which become 'Presse me no more, dear Play, & ile confesse | I loue thee still, nay rather more then lesse.' As the common denominator amongst the source-poems imitated, with the exception of Donne's 'The Broken Heart', is their having been set to music, it seems likely that Goring's original parody was put together from a manuscript song collection which included 'Presse me no more'. The settings for the poems by Suckling and Davenant were by William Lawes. Although no supporting evidence has yet been found, it does not seem improbable that the music for *The Shepherds' Paradise* was composed by one of the Lawes brothers.

There is no evidence of any further performance of the play.

The Tixall Manuscript

The provenance of FTix, apart from a slight uncertainty concerning the exact identity of its first owner, is very straightforward. On the flyleaf at the beginning of the manuscript is written 'The Lady Persalls Booke | borrowed 9^{r} ye 1st 1653'. This appears as an identifying mark in the description of Lot

[44] *Poems*, ed. Rhodes Dunlap (Oxford, 1949), p. 75, ll. 83–8; Paulina Palmer, 'Thomas Carew's Reference to *The Shepherd's Paradise*', *Notes and Queries*, 211 (1966), 303–4; Aurelian Townshend, *The Poems and Masques*, ed. Cedric C. Brown (Reading, 1983), pp. 46–7 (including music by Henry Lawes); Martz, *The Wit of Love*, pp. 87–8. Martz claims that the opening lines of Townshend's poem, 'I have beene in Heav'n, I thinke | For I heard an Angell sing' must derive from Moramante's speech, 'Her soule vseless to her body now is gon to visitt | Heaven, & did salute the Angells wth a song . . .' 3011–12). In the margin beside this speech in FCos 'good' has been written by an appreciative reader.

[45] Goring's poem appears on p. 231b of Bodleian Library MS Rawlinson Poet. 147, a poetic miscellany compiled by Henry Some of Cambridge, probably between 1640 and 1660, but containing a number of 1630s poems. The poems used by Goring include Donne's 'Song (Sweetest love, I do not go)', and 'The Broken Heart', Suckling's Sonnet I ('Dost thou see how unregarded now'), Wither's 'The Author's Resolution in a Sonnet', and Davenant's 'To the Queen Entertained at Night by the Countess of Anglesey'. The originals of three couplets have not been certainly identified, though two lines may be based loosely on a song 'To His Mistress Going to Sea' published by Henry Lawes and attributed to Thomas Cary, son of the Earl of Monmouth. William Lawes also set this to music, but the autograph version in British Library Additional MS 31432 lacks the lines perhaps used by Goring.

597 in the sale by Sotheby's in November 1899 of the library at Tixall (the Staffordshire seat of the Aston family). The library is described in the sale catalogue as 'Late the property of Sir F. A. T. C. Constable BART. (of Burton Constable and Aston Hall, North Ferriby, East Yorks.) FORMED ORIGINALLY BY SIR WALTER ASTON, FIRST LORD ASTON'. Lady Persall is therefore confirmed as being Lady Frances Persall, daughter of Walter Lord Aston, and married some time before June 1635 to Sir William Persall. It is impossible to know whether the manuscript was presented to, or copied for, Lady Persall or her father (or indeed some other member of the family): its being described as her book twenty years after the performance of *The Shepherds' Paradise* cannot be regarded as sufficient corroboration that she was its original owner, as her father did not die until 1639, and her married home was not Tixall but Canwell (also in Staffordshire).

Thereafter the ownership of the manuscript is clear. It was bought on the second day of the Sotheby's sale, 7 November 1899, for twelve shillings by the booksellers Pickering, from whom it passed to George Thorn-Drury, who printed the prologue and songs in his book *A Little Ark*.[46] On his death it was sold again by Sotheby's on 22 February 1932, as Lot 2408, together with FCos which he also owned, to Dobell's, who acquired both manuscripts for £4. 10*s*. The Folger Shakespeare Library bought them from Dobell's at the recommendation of J. Q. Adams in December 1935, FCos for six guineas, and FTix for fifteen.

The Tixall manuscript is a folio bound in parchment-covered boards with traces of two pairs of green silk ties. The title 'The Shepherds' Paradise' has been written in a modern hand on the front cover (which is becoming detached), though the note 'this is the shepards paradi', which appears in italic script upside-down on the centre-right of the base of the cover, is probably contemporary. There are also a number of ink marks on the centre-left of the front cover which suggest someone trying out a pen. 2.5 centimetres from the right-hand edge of the cover, and centrally placed between its head and foot, is a perfectly circular, very neat hole, barely two millimetres in diameter, which goes through the cover and all sheets up to and including Fol. 4, decreasing in size until it disappears. At the base of the spine there is a label which is partially covered by a fragment of paper but possibly reads '203'.

The manuscript consists of 66 leaves measuring 297 mm × 192 mm, made up (as far as it is possible to tell: the leaves are very tightly bound in places) of one single leaf (the flyleaf described above), one gathering of five bifolia, followed by another single leaf, then five gatherings respectively of six, six (or possibly five with a single leaf at each end), one, six and seven bifolia, and two single binding leaves, sewn on to five raised cords. On the paste-down on the inside front cover of the book are two notes, one (presumably by Thorn-Drury) reading 'This differs very much from the other ms. copy which I

[46] George Thorn-Drury, *A Little Ark, Containing Sundry Pieces of Seventeenth-Century Verse* (London, 1921), pp. 4–7.

have. The other copy does not contain the songs between the Acts.', and the other, 'This MS is prepared in the form of a prompt book. J. Q. Adams'. The lower part of the initial flyleaf, which is noticeably grubbier and of poorer quality than the remainder of the paper, is torn away, but at the top of the recto of the leaf is the note referred to above, 'The Lady Persalls Booke | borrowed 9^{r} ye 1st 1653'; it is otherwise blank. The Prologue is on the recto of Fol. 1, and the Scene and *Dramatis personae* on the verso. Act I opens on Fol. 2a, on which the scribe has begun numbering the pages. The pagination is then continuous until the last page of Act V, Fol. 63b (p. 122), including the otherwise blank pages 35b (p. 68) and 48b (p. 92) following the ends of Acts III and IV respectively, but excluding the entirely blank Fol. 37 which follows the Song after the Third Act (Fol. 36a) and a title-page for the fourth act (Fol. 36b). Fols. 36 and 37 form the gathering of a single bifolium noted above. The text of Act II begins on the first, single leaf of the second gathering (Fol. 11a), Act III on the final leaf of the same gathering (Fol. 23a), Act IV on the first leaf of the fifth gathering, and Act V on its final leaf. The foliation for the present edition begins with the first page of text.

Two slightly different versions of a single watermark appear in nearly all of the manuscript. The only exceptions are the final binding leaves, the first of which has a watermark bearing the initials MIV in a single-line box and chain-lines 24–5 mm apart, and the second a five-point Foolscap watermark and chain-lines 25 mm apart. The main watermark is a pot surmounted by a closed crescent, with the letters G/RO on its body. It is found on Fols. 1, 3, 4, 5, 9, 11–14, 17, 19, 20, 24, 27, 30, 31, 33, 34, 36, 44–50, 52, 54–6, 60, and 62. One version appears identical to Heawood 3627 and has chain-lines at a distance of 22–3 mm, while the other is very similar but slightly smaller, with the crescent and the lower curve of the handle both open, and the chain-lines sometimes as close as 18–20 mm.[47] The paper, though slightly browned, is generally in very good condition, except where a chemical used in its composition has caused small scorch marks on its surface, very occasionally leading to the formation of a small hole.

The manuscript is written in a neat, legible hand by a single scribe in a typical Caroline secretary script containing elements of italic. Towards the end the writing becomes larger, looser, and slightly untidy. Italic is always used for speech prefixes and verse, usually for stage directions and catchwords (which always refer to the next spoken word), and sometimes for proper names in the main text. The ink is black, fading to grey.

The scribe appears to have been both careful and accurate in his copying. Seventy-one clear errors unique to FTix have been identified in the textual notes to this edition, but it is impossible to know how many of these were introduced by the scribe or were already present in the manuscript from which he copied. The number of variants arising from the shortening and

[47] Edward Heawood, *Watermarks Mainly of the 17th and 18th Centuries* (Hilversum, 1950). A dilapidated version of the main watermark occurs in a letter in the Folger Shakespeare Library, Xd/483 (49), written from Exeter, 9 February 1650.

rewriting of the text also make it difficult to be certain whether plausible readings found only in FTix are the result of revision or miscopying.

Corrections have frequently been carried out by damping the paper and scraping off its surface, the resulting gap being filled with dashes or flourishes (see Plate 2). At its most successful, this procedure has caused damage to the paper only discernible to the touch, and left no trace of what has been erased. More clumsily applied, it has caused fairly substantial, if very localized, damage. Corrections have twice been made, both in an italic hand in paler ink, in the margin of the manuscript in I. ii, one possibly (line 98) and one certainly (166) by another hand. In line 98 the majuscule *S* of *Setting* is not entirely like that of the scribe, though the remainder of the word is consistent with his writing; and in line 166 *desolue* (which is actually an incorrect correction) is identifiably not by FTix's scribe, who always uses *v* not *u* in this position.

On Fols. 1a, 11a, 24a, 36a, and 50a two pairs of blind vertical parallel lines have been ruled from the recto side with a fairly sharp instrument to create margins. The impression of these is visible on all the following pages (though with decreasing clarity) until the next set of freshly ruled lines. The pair of lines on the left-hand side are on average 15 mm apart, and the further left of the two is 25 mm from the inner edge. Those on the right are 20 mm apart, and the further right of these two is 12 mm from the edge of the page. The text is arranged within the two right-hand lines of each pair (i.e. the inner line of the left-hand pair, and the outer line of the right-hand pair), with dashes and flourishes used to justify the ends of lines. It may have been the existence of the blind-ruled margins which led Adams to identify FTix as a prompt-book, but Bentley is right to point out that 'This manuscript has been creased, and two of the creases used for margins, but the creasing is not according to the system found in several professional prompt manuscripts.'[48] FTix is not a prompt-book: the blind rules are purely for the guidance of the scribe in setting out his text, and there is none of the other identifying features of a working stage manuscript. This was a manuscript prepared for reading.

The Tixall Manuscript and Its Relations

All of the manuscripts of *The Shepherds' Paradise* are scribal copies, none of which is directly related to any other witness; all have marked idiosyncrasies which make them to a greater or lesser degree unsuitable as copy text. The present editor is currently collating the manuscripts and the printed edition for a critical edition of the uncut version of the play, and it is clear that the substantive variants alone will run to many thousands, even before taking into account the revisions in FTix. It is not possible here to do more than indicate major differences between the witnesses, in particular between FTix and the longer texts, and outline the relationship between them.

[48] Bentley, *The Jacobean and Caroline Stage*, iv. 920.

BSt, BPet, and FCos[49] all contain approximately the same quantity of text, and any major variations, additions, and omissions usually amount to only a few lines. The disparity in the number of their lines (5,370, 6,574, and 7,165 respectively) is almost entirely accounted for by differences in the size of the handwriting and the ways in which the texts are set out, with the exception of 160–80 lines lost from the end of Act IV of BSt owing to manuscript damage. BSl, the longest manuscript in terms of text, if not of the number of lines (6,080), contains the Prologue and songs between the acts (an additional 107 lines) otherwise found only in the heavily cut FTix (3,854 lines), as well as a text which is not only uncut but has a small number of lines not found in any other manuscript. Unfortunately, the major of the two scribes who copied it was either very careless or following a very unclear original: speech prefixes are mistaken for the names of people being addressed, with the result that speeches are sometimes misattributed, verse becomes prose, and occasional passages are completely (if interestingly) garbled. Where the same passages of text occur in FTix these errors are not present, although the two manuscripts otherwise have many readings in common. FTix is most closely related to BSl, but has not been adapted directly from it. The evidence suggests that it was copied from an already shortened version, which was abridged and rewritten possibly using the same manuscript from which BSl was copied.

The stemma of *The Shepherds' Paradise* contains two clear branches, one consisting of BSt, BPet, and 8°, the other BSl and FTix. FCos lacks the Prologue and songs found in the latter branch, but does share with it the preliminary description of the scene (that is, where the play is set) and list of *dramatis personae*, not the actresses' cast list found in the former. At the level of individual words, it has many unique readings, but also shares variants with manuscripts on both branches. This would seem to identify it as the earliest of the manuscripts, but while it has other features that might suggest a greater closeness to Montagu's original, there are also elements which indicate that although it was copied from an early state of the text, this was done at a relatively late stage.[50]

BPet is indirectly descended from BSt. They share many single-word variants, but BPet has acquired a number of misreadings, some unique, but many also found in 8°, to which it is very closely related, while BSt has its own omissions and incorrect variants which are absent from BPet and/or 8°. BPet and the printed edition frequently contain variants found in no other witnesses and may be copies of the same lost manuscript. However, an Act V speech which BSt, BPet, and FCos all tack on to the end of the preceding speech is attributed correctly to Genorio only in 8° and BSl (it is cut from

[49] BPet was bought by Quaritch in 1928 in a sale of books and manuscripts from the Percy library at Petworth House, and sold by them to the British Library. FCos belonged to the nineteenth-century collector F. W. Cosens, following whose death in 1890 it was acquired by George Thorn-Drury. Nothing is known of the provenance of BSt and BSl.

[50] FCos is an especially interesting manuscript, not least because a great part of the dialogue is presented in a loose form of blank verse.

FTix). It does not seem obviously enough misplaced for the printer to have made the correction, but until further evidence is available from a systematic collation the relationship between BPet and the printed edition must remain in doubt.

Some of the most significant large-scale variations between different versions of the play concern attempts (whether by Montagu or someone else) to improve Montagu's shaky exposition of the plot. Problems with the identity of Fidamira, with the integration of her supposed father Bonorio ('Bonoso' in FTix only) into the play, with the number of children lost at the siege of Pamplona, and with the need to find a suitable wife for Agenor are repeatedly addressed.[51] The evidence suggests that Montagu may not, at the outset, have intended Fidamira to be sister to Agenor and Bellessa: not until Romero's first appearance half-way through Act V is any reference made to the loss of a second child following the siege, and even then it sounds like an afterthought. In FCos, BSt, and BSl Romero speaks of two of the King of Navarre's children having been lost, describing the disappearance of one (Pallante/Agenor) at Pamplona and the much later flight of another (Saphira/Bellessa) from Navarre. In BPet and 8° the number is increased correctly to three, but only the same two are described. In FTix the speech has been rewritten to include all three lost children (lines 3434–6). However, this greater clarity at the end of FTix is offset earlier in the play: like BSl, it lacks the dialogue concerning Agenor's origins found in all other witnesses at the end of the opening scene, an omission which must have made the plot considerably more opaque for the audience, as would the absence of the brief but problematic scene in Act III (present in BSl, FCos, BPet, and 8°) in which Bonorio gives the audience information on his own identity and relationship to Fidamira.[52] The lack of this scene, along with the cutting of the arrival of Bonorio in the Shepherds' Paradise, means that his appearance in the final scene of FTix in order to reveal his part in the rescue of the infant Fidamira is quite unexplained. Similarly, Fidamira's reference to the King's daughter as being her 'Companion already in what he [the King] knowes not of' (FCos, Fol. 29a)—that is, in loving Agenor—is absent from FTix and BSl, with the result that the arrangement of Arabella's marriage to him in the final scene appears completely arbitrary.[53]

[51] In no version is the Bonorio/Fidamira plot satisfactorily dramatized throughout. A reader would only be able to follow the plot with any degree of ease by having available Acts I and II of FCos, Act III of BPet, and a conflation of Act V from BSt/BPet and FTix.

[52] The scene, if present, would appear in FTix at the end of III. iii, following line 1790. Other manuscripts reveal confusion as to its status: in BSt the scene is signalled by the stage direction 'Enter Bonorio . . . Into a Woode', but the speech itself is missing; in FCos, which alone has a similar scene in Act II, 'Bonorio' has been deleted from the stage direction and replaced by 'Genorio', to whom the speech is attributed; and in BSl the speech is present but the stage direction and speech heading are not.

[53] BPet and 8° have attempted to smooth over this difficulty by the clumsy addition of a conversation between Basilino and Agenor on the fondness for him of the princess, referred to as Arabella in FCos, BSl, and FTix, and Mirabella in BSt, BPet, and 8°.

The obscurities of plot in the early part of FTix are surprising in view of the care that the reviser of FTix has taken to make at least some of Montagu's prose both more intelligible and more forceful. In Votorio's Act II description of the founding of the Shepherds' Paradise, for example, the lines

> Sabina's inclination to *Nauarre* drew downe the power of
> mighty France upon this Prince, to ballance but the hope
> of faire *Sabina*, which he seemed to thinke him selfe a gay-
> -ner by, after the losse of most of his Country;
> (FCos, Fol. 19a)

read, in FTix:

> Sabina's inclination
> to Navarr, drew downe the mighty power of mighty ffraunce vpon
> this Prince: but the hope of faire Sabina (wch he seem'd to thinke
> him selfe a Gayner by, after the losse of most of his Countrey)
> animated him:
> (811–15)

Similarly, in Gemella's Act III 'pretence' for entry to the Society the lines which in FTix read

> The passion of the sonne was first, the fathers followed it,
> vnseene vnto the sonne; The father made the first discovery
> & in a rage resolv'd to cutt of his sonnes life;
> (1696–8)

have been rewritten from

> The passion of the sonne was first,
> The fathers followed it vnseene to the sonne
> of which the father meant to apply the first discouery
> only to benumme and dead what was to be cutt of, his life
> (FCos, Fol. 39b)

The difference in length is negligible, but the gain in sharpness quite considerable. The reviser has worked with great care and precision even at the level of individual words, an exactitude exemplified in the revision from 'this smooth place' to 'that smooth place' (1880) in the King's reference to the Shepherds' Paradise before he reaches it. Evidence from grammatical revisions, as well as stylistic changes, suggests that the reviser was someone other than Montagu. A particularly clear indication is the consistent (though not invariable) alteration of Montagu's characteristic 'so . . . as' construction to 'so . . . that': see, for instance, lines 568–9, 'soe cleere from any staine of selfe=advantage that . . .', where all other texts read 'as'.

These revisions, however numerous, are less striking than those aimed at shortening the text. Two of the uncut manuscripts provide a small amount of evidence as to the process of abridgement, though in both cases this relates to material that was actually retained in FTix.

The meticulous main scribe of FCos has marked passages in Act I which appear to have been considered for omission, and which for the most part do not appear in the BSt/BPet/8° group of texts, but which were included in performance. Fidamira's lines 'And if yor presage . . . benignity of Heaven to you;' (220–4) have been marked in FCos (Fol. 6a, where they constitute six lines) with a long bracket and the word '*Spoke*' in the right margin; these lines are absent from BSt, BPet, and 8°. Similarly, Basilino's 'since I have made . . . separation from you' (308–10; FCos, Fol. 8a, four lines), bracketed without annotation, and Fidamira's 'But sure heaven . . . more refin'd' (420–5; FCos, Fol. 10b, seven lines), enclosed in square brackets with marginal '*Spoken*', are missing from the same witnesses. However, the King's lines in the final speech of Act I 'will love be content . . . prodigious flowers' (649–53), marked in FCos (Fol. 15a, five lines) by a combination of indentation, a long square bracket on the left and brace on the right, and marginal '*spoken*', are present in all versions.

The second set of evidence is clearer, and significant in involving one of the play's most conceptually interesting scenes. Following the vote taken on Gemella's petition to join the Society, in FCos, BSt, BPet, and 8° all votes agree for her admission, and after a short, not wholly relevant speech by her on ambition being contrary to her colour (she is disguised as a Moor), she is sworn in. In FTix (1762–86, Plate 3) Moramante votes against her admission on the grounds that she is so brave that she ought not to have to face the indignity of being debarred because of her colour from being the Paradise's queen. He is severely admonished by Bellessa, who says that beauty is a relative and changing concept, and Gemella is as eligible as the other shepherdesses. There then follows Gemella's now relevant disclaimer to ambition. In BSl, Votorio says, as in FCos, BSt, BPet, and 8°, 'Noe vote opposeth the admission'. Bellessa's 'Whose?' of FTix is missing, but Moramante answers, 'Tis mine Madam', and the rest of the scene then continues more or less as in FTix. Either the scribe of BSl was presented with unclear instructions as to omitting this passage, or failed to understand them.

In the first two acts, any text absent from FTix is, with very few exceptions, also absent from BSl, and the lack of this text is more or less balanced by equal absences in the BSt/BPet branch of the stemma. In I.vi significant material on Moramante's brief conversion to Neoplatonism (508–27) is omitted from all texts except BSl/FTix. In Act III we see the beginning of the major cuts in FTix which occur to a much greater extent in Acts IV and V, but for the most part the omissions in this act consist of only two or three lines each in speeches of between eight and fifteen lines, and proportionately more in longer speeches. The text which has been cut sometimes consists of whole sentences, simply dropped from the end of a speech, but more often the omitted words or lines are skilfully filleted from within a speech and the surrounding sentence linked up. The result usually makes the speech less long-winded and dramatically more effective, but occasionally also produces a change of sense. For example, a cut of six lines from the speech in which Pantamora declares in FTix (2031–42) that 'all the Quarrell I have | now vnto Bellessa is Moromante's love' has the effect of changing the cause of Pantamora's resentment from thwarted ambition to romantic jealousy. Approximately 115 lines have been removed from Act III in this way, and a further sixty in longer cuts, sometimes involving entire speeches. These are concentrated in two scenes: the dialogue between Melidoro and Camena on the nature of love and possession (1626–59), in which Camena's thoughts on the problems suffered by women because of their husbands' concern with masculine honour have been lost; and the discussion between Bellessa, Moramante and Martiro on the possibility of second love (1922–89), from which a degree of repetition has been removed.

If a minor operation has been carried out on Act III of FTix, then radical surgery has been undertaken on Act IV: almost 500 lines have been cut, constituting nearly half the act. The minor abridgements and rewritings typical of Act III still occur, but they are combined with the removal of not only whole speeches but whole scenes. This has the effect of fundamentally altering the balance of the act, particularly in the second half. It is the act in which, in the uncut versions, least action takes place. A subtle flirtation begins between Bellessa and Moramante, to whom Pantamora makes very unsubtle advances; Gemella discovers that Genorio is faithless; and the King sets off for the Shepherds' Paradise. Much of the rest of the act is taken up with discussions as to whether Bellessa is too angelic to love, and if not, whether she is in love with Moramante, together with lengthy disquisitions on the nature of love itself. It is these, for the most part, which have met with the axe, but almost no scene has gone unpruned. The extent of the cuts is not immediately apparent, as Act IV opens with one of the scenes between Moramante and Bellessa which throughout the act remain least liable to major omissions, and the following scenes between Moramante and Pantamora, Moramante and Genorio, and Genorio and Gemella (FTix, 2442–568) are also relatively untouched. Following Gemella's exit (2577), however, a soliloquy by Martiro on the impossibility of Bellessa's ever being in love has been dropped, and the discussion between Melidoro and Camena (2681–708), which in the uncut versions offers us one of the play's most detailed expositions of Neoplatonic love, has been abridged by more than half, to leave a short conversation which concentrates on the personal—who is in love with whom—at the expense of the ideal. The following scene, in which Martiro reads his poem on impossibility, has only one significant cut: the second half of the poem has simply been dropped (2768–81). After this point the axe really descends. A long dialogue (100 lines) between Genorio and Gemella on inconstancy is omitted, as well as the subsequent fifty-line dialogue in which Genorio attempts to discover the state of play between Moramante and Bellessa. Pantamora's and Gemella's soliloquies (2810–40) – which appear in FTix in the opposite order to that found in all other texts – have been cut almost in half, and the whole of the eighty-line scene which follows, in which Bellessa, Martiro and Gemella discourse on vanity and love, has been removed.

Almost half the text has similarly been cut in Act V, in this case amounting to approximately 1000 lines. Again, the parts of Bellessa and, to a lesser extent, Moramante, have lost the fewest lines, while the roles of Genorio and the King have been cut to their bare essentials and Martiro, Melidoro and Camena have been almost entirely removed from Act V. About a quarter of the lines have been lost in an elimination of all the small scenes (involving mainly the minor characters) which occur in the uncut texts between Gemella's dialogue with Bellessa (3472–95; largely rewritten in FTix) following the latter's return from Love's Cabinet, and the final long multiple recognition scene (3496–858), but there is no scene, and scarcely a speech, which has not been affected by cuts. The stripping away of repetition and compliment has the result of producing a considerably more readable—possibly even stageable—play, but some of the passages lost, such as Camena's arguments as to why a woman would prefer to stay single, or Melidoro's mockery of Genorio's new-found Neoplatonism, have their own interest in terms of contemporary court culture, and the loss of almost all argument and reflection may not always be such an improvement for the reader as it presumably was for the actors and audience.

Editorial Conventions

This is a near-diplomatic transcription, in which the following conventions have been observed. Square brackets enclose deletions, except those around folio numbers ([Fol. 6a], etc.). Angle brackets enclose material which other causes (paper damage, blotting) have removed or made difficult or impossible to decipher. In such cases, dots indicate illegible characters (thus <.>)]. Deletions made by damping and scraping off the top layer of paper, causing paper damage, have been indicated by enclosing within angle and square brackets the dashes or flourishes used to cover the gap created by the deletion (thus [<~~>]). Such deletions are also recorded in the textual notes. Interlined words are enclosed within half brackets (thus 787, ⌜the say of⌝), and all interlineations are recorded in the notes. Carets are not printed, but their presence is noted. Differences in the size of italic hand have been regularized: one large size is used for act and scene headings, speech prefixes, and continuous pieces of italic text such as the Prologue and songs (with the exception of the Scene and *Dramatis personae* (Fol. 1b), where two sizes are clearly distinguished by the scribe), and a smaller one, the same size as the main roman text, for italic words occurring within the text. Italicized stage directions are normally in the larger print except where they are plainly written in the same size as the main text, usually where they occur at the end of a line. Words are printed in italic where all or most of the letters are clearly written in an italic hand. The name 'Moromante' is peculiarly problematic in this respect, as the first half of the word is often italic, while the second is more obviously in secretary script. In this case an editorial judgement has been made as to which script is dominant.

Each line of text—including act and scene divisions, speech prefixes, and stage directions—is numbered separately. Catchwords, rules, decorations, page numbers, and interlineations of one or two words are excluded from the line count. Numbering for the text is continuous, and begins with the Prologue on Fol. 1a. The text is printed without a break in this edition, but it should be noted that the scribe has allotted new pages to all of the Songs between the Acts, the title pages for Acts II, III, and IV, and the Ceremony at the Tombs. Omitted from the text, but recorded in the collations, are markings not intended as part of the transcript (ink blots, pen marks, etc.). The position of elements of the text such as speech-prefixes, headings, catchwords, page numbers, and indented text is reproduced as exactly as type permits, but other features are normalized.

Several letter shapes require editorial decisions, especially in distinguishing between majuscule and minuscule forms, in particular where the scribe uses an intermediate form of initial *L* for significant words within sentences (for example, 414 'Love', 1528 'Lawes'). These have normally been transcribed as majuscule. Similar judgements have to be made concerning the suspension of letter forms in the abbreviations 'wch'/'w^{ch}' and 'wth'/'wth'. In some cases the intention to raise letters is made unmistakable by the presence of a full stop under the superscript letters, but more often the central letter lifts slightly above the level of the text, then the loops of the secretary *h* come down again to their normal placement on the line; these have been transcribed without suspension. Superscript letters have been printed the same size as the rest of the text. Marked irregularities in word division are recorded in the collations, but not in those frequent instances which are a result of the scribe failing to remove his pen from the paper. Apostrophes are printed as written, even where superfluous or wrongly placed. The position of punctuation above or below the line has been normalized. The longer strokes or virgules which the scribe used to end speeches are printed in the text, as are the dashes and flourishes used to fill spaces at the ends of the justified lines. The abbreviations for *er/ar*, *per/par* and *pro* have been expanded, and shown in the text as italic (thus 189 p*ro*claime, 194 p*ar*t). Other contractions and tildes are printed as they appear in the manuscript, except where the scribe has shown the abbreviation of words ending in '-con' by curling the last stroke of the *n* back over the preceding letters; this has been represented by a line above the end of the word. Long *s* has been lowered and terminal *s* rendered as *s* rather than *es*, even where the letter resembles the common abbreviation for *es/is*. Ligature *æ* has been retained.

Scribal mistakes are recorded in the textual footnotes. Where the incorrect reading is unique to the Tixall manuscript, and all other manuscripts share the correct reading, a correction is provided, to the right of the lemma, from only FTix's closest relative, British Library Sloane MS 3649 (BSl) (thus 184 *afixid*] *afraid* BSl). Where these two (or more) manuscripts share the mistake, the correction is given from all witnesses in which it appears in the order in which they are most closely related to FTix, though showing the spelling of only the first witness cited (thus 434 *affection*] *affliction* FCos, BSt, BPet, 8°; 480 *note*] *vote* FCos, BPet, 8°). Where there is more than one possible correction, all of them are listed (thus 3057 *Thy*] *The* FCos; *My*

BSt, BPet, 8°). In the very heavily cut and rewritten second half of the play, where corrections are more problematic, the ends of sentences which have been oddly shortened have twice been supplied in the notes (2242, 2956). A full-scale collation, which would consist of thousands of variant readings, has not been attempted.

The pages in Plates 1–4 have been reproduced four-fifths full size.

Diana: What newes Apollo, from the Highest spheres.
The noyse is such, that it hath toucht my ears;

Apollo: Happy Diana, whome the Gods agree
Mistris of what they all doe long to see.
The Beauty of this night: all knowing Jove
Would have stole downe, arm'd wth. the God of Love;
But Juno iealous wth more reason now
Then ere before, would not this stealth allow;
This quarrell made the subiect of it knowne,
Then every one of them would have come downe;
This equall envy keepes them all away,
For none even to be left King, there would stay;
Soe now by this they all consented are,
Each one to put himselfe into a Starre:
And thus in Gallantry each brings a light,
And waites wth. it, a servant to this night,
They'le give the light & leave you to preside,
In vertue, but as you are Deifide:
This is resolv'd above, & I am sent
Hither from all, to make this Complement; //

Diana: Heaven could have chose (Apollo) none soe fitt,
As you the God of Harmony & witt,
Juno did well, her husband would have seene,
A Paradise contain'd in such a Queene:
He might have own'd this as his propper place
Alledging Heaven was truly in her face.
And all the other Gods might have staid here,
Where each one might have found a severall sphaere:
So lovely & soe heavenly=resembling Eyes
Might have made good their leaving of the Skyes;
You will beleive your Eyes but 'twill distresse
Even your divinest Eloquence to expresse.
What you shall see, lets yeild now to their light
wch would have made me seeme but a cloud of night;
Let vs together then, now both retire,
And ioy that wee are Gods, but to admire; //

Shepheards Paradise

PLATE 1: FOLGER SHAKESPEARE LIBRARY MANUSCRIPT Vb 203,
FOL. 1a, LINES 1–36

She enioyed the Regency during her life, & then left the propriety of all vnto the Queene; wch is elegible as you haue heard; The peace & settlednes of this place is secur'd by nature, Inclosure of it, on all sides by inpregnablenes, as if it was meant for Chastity only to make a plantation here; at one passage only the Rockes seeme to open themselues, wch is maintayn'd by a Garrison of the Kings, wch deliuer all strangers to be as Sutors, not Inuadors; Thus haue I inform'd you of the institution of this order, wch was call'd by the Foundresse The Shepheards Paradice, as being a peacefull receptacle of distressed mindes, & sanctuary agt. fortunes seuerest executions: Now Sr. I must needs tell you the generous end of the Prince of Nabarr, that you may see there was nothing accessary to this heauenly institution, that had not a transcendant wonder of brauery; The Prince (as it seemes, hating that earth, whose safety hath occasion'd his losse of Sabina) in scorne of it, forsooke it, & came hither in a disguise, & was admitted into the order; where he liu'd conceal'd, & dying wthout euer making himselfe knowne to Sabina: but at his death left such a notorious memory: as all ages, ages shall study to blazon it, & put it to the royallest ornamt. that can be due to Princes; The Queene ordain'd a particular Ceremony to be perform'd euery yeare at this Tombe, wch is iustly obseru'd;

Mor: This is soe heauenly a Tradition, as it becomes best yor. deliuery; This order seemes a match betweene loue, honour & Chastity, wch you are happy Sr. being the Preist to; but giue me leaue to wonder why the brothers are excluded out of the election, wch is to bee guided most by beauty; of wch sure they are best Iudges;

Coto: The reason Sr. that I haue heard was then giuen by the Foundresse; that it had bin to haue made them Iudges in their owne Causes: since there is noe man, but hath a particuler interest that doth prepossesse his choyce; whereas all women are rather Inquisitors, then Admirators one of another, & being voyd of passion noe freindshipp, can incline them to yeild priority in beauty: & so 'twas thought most probable, & where most of them agreed to yeild, the advantage must be vnquestionable;

Mor: The wisdome Sr. of the Foundresse was such, as it carryes away our Admiration, euen wth this our prouidence: I haue one satisfaction more to desire of you, wch the omission of I doe beleiue (in yor. opinion) render me vnworthy of those I doe already owe: The knowledge of this your now Queenes Condition; & the time of her admission & her preferment;

His

PLATE 2: FOL. 13a, LINES 845–85

night, And that there did remaine noe time for him
to doe any thing but fly, this he beleiving did flye --
instantly; wch I assur'd of, my next part was now to un-
maske my vertue whose vizard was offensive; Therefore
winged wth innocence I did resolve to flye, over those seas
wch yt our neighbouring Islands: leaving a letter wch
might cleare my vertue, from that black Suspicion I
had made: comming hither the kind Gods presented me, wth
the report of this Divine abode, wch offers it selfe equally
to the releife of all the distrest of all Nations & sexes;
Thus have you heard a story whose strangeness needs sommons
your pitty, it must first aske yor Creditt, as a Charity: wch if
you vouchsafe, I cannot doubt a faire Consideration;

Queen: Votorio Collect the votes.
[He Collects them & sayes]

Voto: Noe vote opposeth the Admission, but one.
Queen Whose?
Moram: Tis mine Madam, that doth dissent only for a fitter pitty
to this unhappy Lady, for she seemes arm'd wth a minde
brave enough not to esteeme this residence an ease, that
shall exclude her from the Dignity of the Queene; wch
her selfe wee know doth debarr her here being a Moore;
if she can lett her selfe fall into these Conditions, shee
shall have my vote, to be more pittyed after her admission
then before;
Queen: You have fayl'd Moromante in both parts.

Can nature be accus'd of spight
for having made both day & night
That wch is inur'd by Comparison,
Must be Comparable or can have none,

She

57

PLATE 3: FOL. 27a, LINES 1747–76

She sings:

Presse me noe more kind love, I will confesse
And tell you all, nay rather more then lesse;
Soe youle assure me when I're told you, then
Not to bring me to witnes it to men:
Though thus you're strong enough to make me speake
Held by the virgin shame you'l be too weake,
I finde that thus, I may be safely free;
Best by this freedome, I ingag'd may bee;
I find a glowing heat that turnes red hott,
My heart, but yet it doth not flame a iott.
It doth but yet to such a Colour turne,
It seemes to me rather to blush then burne,
you would perswade me that a flaming light
riseing will change this Colour into white,
I would faine in this whity inference:
Pretend pale guilt or Candid Innocence:
If you will tell me wch wthout deceipt.
I will allow you light, aswell as Heat.

I finde a gentle drowsynes slyp o're my senses as if my thoughts had wearyed them: [Shee sleepes

Moromante:

Mor: was it the rapture that my soule is alwayes in, when it Contemplates the Divine Bellesta, that did p'sent her voyce unto me there in Heaven! Sure it was! [Hee sees her asleepe & stands wondring

Her soule woke to her body now, is gon to visitt Heaven, & did salute the Angells wth a song, Lett sleepe noe longer be call'd death's Image, here is an animation of it, sure all the life that sleepe takes from the rest of the world, hee hath brought hither & lives here [He goes nearer her] Doth the

-96

PLATE 4: FOL. 50b, LINES 2985–3017

Diana: *What newes Apollo, from the Highest sphæres.* [FOL. 1a]
The noyse is such, that it hath toucht my eares;

Apollo: *Happy Diana, whome the Gods agree.*
Mistris of what they all doe long to see.
The Beauty of this night: all knowing Iove.
Would have stole downe, arm'd wth the God of Love;
But Iuno iealous, wth more reason now
Then e're before, would not this stealth allow;
This quarrell made the subiect of it knowne,
Then every one of them would have come downe;
This equall envy keepes them all away,
For none even to be left King, there would stay;
Soe now by this they all consented are,
Each one to put himselfe into a starre:
And thus in Gallantry each brings a light,
And waites wth it, a servant to this night,
They'le give the light, & leave you to preside,
In vertue, but as you are Deifide;
This is resolv'd above, & I am sent.
Hither from all, to make this Complement; //

Diana: *Heaven could have chose (Apollo) none soe fitt,*
As you the God of Harmony & witt;
Iuno did well, her husband would have seene,
A Paradise, contain'd in such a Queene:
He might have own'd this as his propper place
Alledging Heaven was truly in her face;
And all the other Gods might have staid here.
Where each one might have found a severall sphære:
So lovely & soe heavenly=resembling Eyes
Might have made good their leaving of the skyes;
You will beleive your Eyes but 'twill distresse
Even your divinest Eloquence to expresse.
What you shall see, lets yeild now to their light,
wch would have made me seeme but a cloud of night;
Let vs together then, now both retire,
And ioy that wee are Gods, but to admire; //

18 *Deifide*] *D* altered from *b* 29 *heavenly*=] *heauen*= BSl

The Scæne Gallica: [Fol. 1b]

The Actors a Society of Shepheards reduced vnder Lawes & to a Governement of their owne by consent of the King and graunt of many priviledges, being govern'd by a Queene of theire owne election. //

Dramatis personæ

King of Castile
Basilino, the Prince, called in his disguise Moramante
Fidamira his Mistris called in her disguise Gemella,
Agenor his freind called in his disguise Genorio;

Votorio –	*A Preist*
Timante *Osorio* }	*Twoe Courtiers*
Bellessa –	*The Shepheards Queene.*
Martiro *Melidoro* }	*Twoe Shepheards*
Camæna *Pantamora* }	*Twoe Shepheardesses*

Romero a Lord of Navarr, father to Martiro,
Bonoso a Lord of Castile supposed father to Fidamira,

Actus I · *Scaena* · I ·

[Fol. 2a]

Osorio, Timante,

Osor: What whisper's this Timante, that awakes our Prince out of his Amorous slumber, & blowes him thus abroad, to seeke for rest in agitation?

Timant: This noyse *Osorio*, hath past by my Eares: But iudge you how vnfitt to be let into our beleifes, when it may be a womans vertue, thats of proofe ag^{t} such power of youth & honor as our matchles Prince — attempts wth, whose repulse must Councell his retreate;

That cannot be soe Osorio, Constancy would toomuch cheapen her ⌢ vertue, should she impart such a p*ro*portion of her selfe vnto a woman: when the rarity of it in that sex is that wch hath raised Constancy to such a vertue.//

Oso: There's a Degree of vertue women may obteine in their defence wch they reteyne even after they are taken: ag^{t} Princes assaults there's nothing to be required in a neglect of speedy Composicon; for taken as – 'twere by assault, they remaine wth asmuch hono^{r} as women were borne to, ffidamira hath already made such a resistance, that it – almost confirmes the possibility of a womans defending of herselfe ag^{t} a Prince: there now her surrender is a Trophie to her; And the Gods owe - - that satisfaccon (the dishonour of ffidamira) to the ⌢ vertuous Princesse of Navarr; who they say quit their ffathers love in iust disdaine to marry any one that lov'd another; I am sorry the Prince is guilty of an Iniury to soe excellent a Creature:

Tim: Looke *Osorio* where the Prince & ffidamira come, Their lookes mee thinckes imply soe litle peace, as even their sorrowes seeme to contend for Mastery:

Oso: Come let's retire Timante, wee shall know what kind of stormes these Cloudes containe.

Exeunt:

66 *may*] *must* BSl 71 *hath*] loop of ^{1}*h* blotted *Constancy*] *anc* corrected in blacker ink, with slight paper damage beneath; corrected letters indecipherable, right-slanting pen-stroke above *a* 73 *of*] tail of *f* blotted, with some paper damage 74 *there's*] ^{2}*e* blotted 75 *in*] *but* BSl 80 *owe*] has been added later in a space too long for it, and the gap filled with horizontal strokes; ink heavier, written with a thicker nib 81 *their ffathers love*] *her ffath*^{rs} *Court* BSl 81–2 *in iust*] cramped, *in* small and poorly formed, *iust* in too small a space

Scena · 2 ·
Basilino, ffidamira;

Basil: Gentle ffidamira, forgive these words & lookes that come in mourning to Demaund Albrizias of you for their newes; The vse I meane to – make of this my heavynes, is but to sinke me downe into a Levell – even wth you, That from thence you may receive a resolution from your equall, not your Prince, But in this divesture of my selfe, I finde a reall Ornament, that reason Clothes me wth, richer & easyer then those shadowes I put off of *Prince* [<- - ->] & powerfull, me thinkes I find an activenes in all my thoughts, they rest not now betweene their telling *Setting* forth, & heaven, where they find Iustice soe inthron'd, as it must needs affect power wth an emulation to be such;

This

I)

This sight I owe your vertue, for in pursuit of that wch fled before me [FOL. 2b] vp to heaven for safety, my thoughts were carryed thither, & detain'd & were thus blest for following you: And (there indeed forgiven) now I may iustlyer resume the name of Prince thus given by you; & yet reserve disparity betweene vs, for my becoming thus a Prince, p*ro*ves you an Angell, And that prompts me to a Demaund, wch I doe aske because it is the greatest blessing mortality can tast, & consequently you only can impart; for sure I was not destin'd, to owe you lesse, then all the good that you can give;//

ffidam: If I were sad before Sr for one attempted Innocence, I might bee – much more now, for this soe generall iniury to all our sex, in wch you seeme Sr [but] to exalt ⌜but⌝ a resistance of vnruly wishes, to that height of vertue our sex can rise to; Nor is it insolence in me, to be indued wth noe lesse then all these prayses that such a breath may seeme to Challenge, since I thinke the occasion worthy of – none but that wch is due to the Gods; for the effect of wch you ascribe to it your owne Conversion vnto vertue, wch p*ro*miseth a further – – app*ro*bation of that wch I ⌜my selfe⌝ shall thinke [<–>] Comendable: Nothing can be called Temptation Sr to Innocency, to make itselfe

92 *Demaund*] *D* altered from *t*   97] erasure damage covered by three horizontal strokes   98 *telling*] lightly underlined with two crosses above, the correction *Setting* (possibly in another hand) added in the margin, all in paler ink   100 *such*] *iust* BSl   101 *me*] in margin   103 *there indeed*] *their intent* BSl   111 *sex,*] ? comma; could be pen mark   112 [1]*but*] deleted by heavily inked line, letters barely legible following erasure damage to the paper   [2]*but*] interlined with caret   118 *my selfe*] interlined with caret   118] erasure damage to paper, no letters visible, space filled with single thick horizontal line

away; All's lost in the possessing, but such a vertue as should dare resist a Princes faire & hono^rable love, when the yeilding is a — victory: such a bravery of vertue were a subiect worthy of yor prayse;
To what a height of Contemplation would such a subiect rayse your soule, wch, the p^rservacon but of Innocence hath carryed even already into heaven: //

Basil: Sure ffidamira, vertue is not neere such an extreame, vertue is alwayes gentle, & pliant to the strength of reason: it weakens it selfe when it hardens into obstinacy, what reason can vertue bring wth it to iustefy it selfe, in the neglect of soe fitt an exercise of it selfe, as is a Princes faire & vertuous Love?

ffidam: It must p*ro*duce that wch is above all reason, faith, either to the Gods, or men: vertue p^rserves her temper in her tendernes of either of these vowes, nor can a Prince bring any reason that this vertuous tendernes may not o'reflow.

Basil: ffaith to the Gods ffidamira is scarce a good excuse for dispaire; how can it then p*ro*tect a froward Contempt, of all the Ioyes & blessings the Gods ordaine for those that represent themselves;
And faith to men cannot be soe religious as not to be subiect to soe high a dispensation: might it not remitt it selfe, even Constancy might soe become a sinne: No ffidamira heaven hath not left such

a temptacon

2.)

a temptacon for Princes to repine, as a p*er*mission of such a – frowardnes to defeate their iust desires; [FOL. 3a]

ffidam: I wonder not to see a Prince somuch mistaken in this vertue, ⌢ Constancy, that is soe free that Tirranny enlargeth it, Princes ⌢ should doe well to prove it to be noe vertue, since it may warrant disobedience to them: Nor have you (that call yor selves the Images of the Gods) reason to repine, that in yor large Comission they have reserved the soveraignty of our wills vnto themselves; you then; – (young Prince) that have inthron'd your selfe among the Gods, by the confinement of yor wishes to be iust, knowe there are none soe that would distresse, much lesse, breake a p*ro*mis'd faith;

Basil: By these turning steps I shall winde my selfe into an admiration of

132 *above*] written as *a bove* 134 *these*] ^I*e* heavily inked 135 *o'reflow.*] pen rest above full stop gives appearance of colon 145 *Tirranny*] *i* heavily blotted

her; soe as I shall not wonder at her refusall; 'tis time to goe directly to my wishes, that they may be the more conspicuous: what I can plead to be prferr'd by, is your making me more happy then any other:

ffidam: Oh how blest am I! that have the meanes to make soe brave a — Prince happyer then he can wish;

Basil: Noe more my ffidamira; I won't exact a word more then is — necessary for a consent;

ffidam: Sr I must expound this happines to you, you will not vnderstand it els: ffirst know Sr I love you soe, that I ioy to thinke that you may leave soe new & vnmatch't an example of yor vertue as my ~//– strange Condicon doth: Know Sr I have deposited my faith, & have received a mutuall pawne vpon it; & it must be yor anger sooner then yor love, that may selove it; And were it not a blemish to your Innocence, even Death would be an ease to mine; (*she kneeles*) But pardon (Royall Prince) even this litle digression into a Doubt of you; The Gods that would not have your vertues call'd in question by a feare, assure me already you will by a forgivenes of mee, ⌢ possesse yor selfe of a Diviner happines then can be gain'd by any acquisition;

de+solue

Basil: Oh doe not mocke me thus in a submisse delivery of the sentence of the iustest heavens, in wch you have but Angells p*ar*t, to be the bearer of it, to make the guilty fire of my lust, to be the refiner of your vertue for anothers vse; But I find Heaven mercifull in this that it vouchsafes me a miracle for Consolacon aswell as punishmt, That an accession of my love to ffidamira should – bring a patience wth it to consent to this perpetuall distance you have now p*ro*nounc'd, All meritt to you ffidamira in this separation from my selfe to this exalted patience I disclaime, & owne my –

badd

3.)

[Fol. 3b]

bad humanity in my afflixion for this; But I will p*ro*mise you the rest of my sad life shalbe imployed, to study this hard happines, wch is not at the first soe easily vnderstood: But I'm afixid ye thoughts of you (wch must be alwayes mixed wth my studyes) will keepe it long obscure;

ffidam: Oh that I were young Prince, what you have call'd me, but in my

154 *directly*] *ectly* cramped   166 *selove*] lightly underlined, correction *desolue* in another hand in margin, *des* similarly underlined with cross above   *desolue*] *release* BSl   174 *Angells part*] *an* ~ BSl   184 *easily*] *ea* altered   *afixid*] *afraid* BSl

excuse an Angell, that I might flye through all the Quarters of the world, & wth Angells voyce p*ro*claime the yet vnheard of vertues of the matchles *Basilino*: The grossest part of the earth (where love's soe over growne wth fflesh, as it is not to be knowne) would shake it selfe apeices at my voice; And love abstracted, growne it selfe, would soe remaine in emulation at our praise; But for your p*ar*t of happines, you seeme not yet to see it; If you must know S^{r} this is none of those light colour'd Ioyes, wch fade & sully in the handling; This is one, wch wearing setts a glosse & lustre on; wch can't decay but by yor leaving of it of, & still the more y^{u} thinke on me, even those sad thoughts, wilbe true shadowes to set off yor ioyes:

Basil: I must no longer ffidamira trust my Infant vertue ag^{t} the ⌢ – growing strength of all thy Beautyes; wch imp*ro*ve in this my [<~>] interdiction of them; I'le leave you ffidamira & wthout asking any thing; not somuch as whoe is the subiect, somuch rather then the Prince, by the consignm^{t} of yor faith; And I doubt but the heavens thinke me soe fully punisht, as they will ne're consent vnto the breach of this my vow, of never being guilty – even of the indirectest sollicitation of your love: And some – auspitious Deity, Antedates this ease vnto me, in the beleife that noe other man shall ere enioy the matchles ffidamira:,

ffidam: Goe worthy Prince, & may you leave me all yor sorrowes, may yor Triumphant youth be crown'd wth such successe, in all our future wishes, as that the pleasing multitude may p*er*swade you, you had never fail'd in any: And may you ne're – – – remember me, till yor glorious life, glutted with prayses of out doing all, yor sex may looke back on me for a more transcendant honour, by this marke of how much you have out done your selfe: //

And

4)

[FOL. 4a]

And soe p^{r}sent you wth an vnhop'd for ioy, wch is the onely — retribution I can make you: Till then, let me & sinne bee att distance from yor thoughts; And if yor p^{r}sage S^{r} hath bespoke my fortune, I shall beleive that heaven (that can't admitt of

192 *apeices*] *a* and *p* joined with a pen stroke, but far enough apart to be intended perhaps to be two words
193 *our*] *yor* BSl 202] erasure damage, no letters visible, space filled with pen flourish 203 *rather*] *richer* BSl
204 ^{1}*the*] *his* FCos, BSt, BPet, 8° 207 *indirectest*] ink heavy and smudged on *t*, probably owing to a correction
211 *our*] *your* BSl 219–20 *att distance*] ~ *a* ~ FCos, BSt, BPet, 8°

breach of ffaith) doth vouchsafe to suspend the execucon of it, for the reward of your meritorious patience; And soe be pleas'd wth the assurance of the benignity of Heaven to you;

Basil: *ffare* well (faire maide) you shall soone heare of resolutions shall some way deserve those good wishes you have now advanc'd;

ffidam: May all the blessings that I could wish you (wch are vnexp^{r}ssable) fall downe as wonders on you; *Exeunt.*

Scena · 3 · Agenor sol:

Agen: The Prince stayd long wth ffidamira, & is now going hastily vnto the king: his lookes, me thought imply'de some strange resolve; – He purpos'd now to make his last attempt, & to venter even his Crowne to take my ffidamira; who's vertue's such, as I beleive her beuty was bestowed vpon her only to p*ro*vide a tryall of it, ⌢ worthy of her glorying in, & the earth hath not a fitter, then the iust offers of this worthy Prince; Oh here he comes; *(En: Basil:)*

Basil: Oh my Agenor, had I now leisure equall to my sence of ffidamira's goodnes, I should not deferr a minute from the makeing thee admire her too, Agenor: she hath made me happyer then I did hope; I am resolv'd Agenor, & I have already soe dispos'd the King my father, as I beleive this second time shall carry his consent; Come Agenor, Let's not loose a minute in't;

Agen: Stay I beseech you S^{r} a while, that I may be acquainted wth your will; & soe know how to argue for you:

Basil: Come away Agenor, I'le tell you as wee goe, The King may 'chance intend t'imploy yor Credit wth me to diswade mee, but I'le convince you by the way;

Agen: I shall but reele a long betweene my shaking feare & shakeing trust of ffidamira; *Exeunt.*

Scena: 4:
King: Osorio: Timante:

King: Leave vs all; how much allay have all Princes Treasures in

223 *patience*] *nc* blotted 233 *ffidamira;*] could be comma with pen mark above 234 *beuty*] for *beauty* 246 *t'imploy*] written as one word

them! even those that are ordain'd for blessings to come themselves,
their Children;

Even

5)

Even these rich Images doe sometimes p*ro*ve burdens, not ~ – [Fol. 4b]
treasures to them: I am in this distresse,
The name of King wch doth exalt the [bl..ss....] blessing of a father,
is only that wch doth forbid me the indulgency of a father,
were he intirely mine, I could let my Iudgem^{t} fall into a Complacency
of this his wish; But as I am, as it were his Guardyan, accomptant
to all my Kingdome for him, I must not expose this estate to such
a hazard as his absence; when I seeme but to stand p*ro*pt vp by him:
I am resolv'd to offer him, rather to quitt the thought of the — –
Princesse of Navarr, & to give him my consent to marry ffidamira,
whome they say he loves wth a passion, able to controll his reason
much more his follies;

[*Enter Basil: & Agenor,*

I have [b] my Basilino bin soe affected with thy wishes, as when
by the p*er*vsall of my collected thoughts, I could find noe reason
to approve of thy intended sep*ar*ation from vs, I did addict them all
to search for an excuse of the Indulgence of my consent, And
thou art soe vnhappy in thy birth, as I have multitudes to satisfy,
on whome reason it selfe can seldome have it's operation; much lesse
a naturall tendernes can move ag^{t} it; In what a strange distresse
am I whom reason doth appoint to displease him in the world I
lov'd best for others satisfac$\overline{con}$; for my owne interests (wch are such
as I cannot repeate wthout reproaching Basalino of vnnaturalnes
in soe p^{r}ferring his owne before them) I will by silence give them
leave to passe by, & remitt them all into his owne power, as a –
suitor, not a Iudge; & for my p*ar*t doe make the King of this
thy wish by my consent;
But I make you thus a King, Basilino, that you might have ~ ⌢
something worthy a ffathers asking; & that the disposition of this

253 *come*] *coine* BSl *themselves*] cramped 257] paper damage suggests that an attempt at complete erasure was made before deletion with a single thick line; the deleted word appears to have read *blessing*, but presumably contained a no longer discernible error 259 *Complacency*] cramped 264 *ffidamira*] *amira* cramped 268 *[b]*] eyeslip from *bin* 273 *seldome*] ^{2}*e* blotted 276 *lov'd*] *loue* FCos, BSt, BPet, 8° 280 *make*] *ke* visible beneath blot

yor wish, might ⌜be⌝ yor guift to me, not my refusall of it; And now I doe conire you Basilino, by the power of a King that hath – – depos'd himselfe, rather to pray, then to com̄aun̄d; to change this your desire of leaving vs, into any other you can thinke of; & stay here still; this shalbe esteemed the greatest blessing that I & my Kingdome are capable off;

Basil: Oh that the angry Gods would pitty me somuch that I might obey you in a fatall silence; It is not a feathred fancy that carryes me to fly above yor will but a well weigh'd misfortune wch beares me downe before you to demaund ease of my oppression: wch I must have some time & distance to discharge my selfe of;

6)

Nor

[Fol. 5a]

Nor hath any Eares been soe defective in any Circumstance, as to distract me quite, & soe free from the sence of all yor interests: but it seemes to admitt an insensiblenes of all my owne to keepe me – wholly for the surview of yours: whose contradiction of my Ease is the refineds't torment; But I could provide by Ingagem^{t} to you S^{r} ag^{t} any important p^{r}iudice my absence may but threaten; Of my arrivall & my residence in every severall place, you shall be certefyde: And my p*ro*mise to retorne to you on any Sum̄ons, wch shall report but even yor feares, may secure you from any – p^{r}iudice of my distance, wch I would Condition should not be out of the lymitts of ffraunce or Spaine; Now S^{r} have pitty of one whome you have rob'd of prayer, by making him a King ag^{t} his will; ⌢ And thinke this submission of my selfe vnto you wilbe a sacrifice worthy of a father & a King to value, since I have made noe – scruple of my misery: I have convinc'd all those publicke and paternall reasons you have alleadged ag^{t} my separation from you: But for your large offer S^{r} I am soe resolv'd, I had but this one thing to aske of you, the wch (to ease you S^{r}) I am content to deny my — selfe;

The Prince wthdrawes sadly.
The King speakes to Agenor.

King: Oh Agenor is not Basilino vniust too, to add vnto my sorrowes by his sharing wth me in them? into what a parralell of misery are – wee both come, by this our meeting one another;

284 *be*] interlined with caret 285 *conire*] for *coniure* 291 *silence;*] possibly a colon 294 *some time*] written as *sometime* 295 *any Eares*] *my eares* BSl; *my Curse* FCos, BPet, 8°; *my care* BSt 296 *free*] ~ *me* BSl 316 *too,*] not in BSl 317 *are*] *a* corrected from *h* or *b*

Agen: In this agreemt Sr where yor misfortunes meete & not yor wishes A subiect may interpose himselfe, & breake of the Accord; I doe not see Sr how the hazard of the Princes desires, equalls that of yours: you endanger Sr the losse of your owne wish in the possessing of it; ffor you shall rather keepe a Prisoner then a sonne; And by his ⌢– liberty on the Conditions he hath p*ro*posed, you shalbe more secur'd then by his residence wth you: The fame of him in all yor neighboring Nations, shall make your people thinke that he is a Prince of them too, & feare you more; Therefore my opinion is that you consent to his first choyce, vpon those termes wch hee him selfe desires it;

King There is Agenor such a Darkenes spread over Basilino, as o'recasts my reason, & cleares vp his to me; methinkes I see this his obedience set so heavy on him, as it oppresseth me, for whome he offers to sinke vnder it; No Basilino thou shalt not thus acquit thy selfe of all those obligations I can challenge as a father & a King, by this out suffering all the benefitts, that even those names can e're conferr;

Throwe

7)

He goes toward Basilino [Fol. 5b]

Throw of my Basilino the supposition of these Clouds that hange vpon thee; thou art deceiv'd if thou beleev'st thy lookes are darke or or'ecast; The bright obedience of thy soule shines through – them, & hath dissol'vde those Clouds that shadowed me; into these drops wch fall now but like Sunshine showers in signe of fairer weather; Therefore now (vpon this Caution of thy so full obedience) I may venter Basilino to call thee any thing: & I will keepe thee in this the Exercise of this thy vertue; Therefore I com̄aund thee now to enioy the first choyce of thy intended travell, vpon what Conditions thy owne direction shall make when thou art gone, & not before; It were a sin not to reward thy duty wth full liberty, wherefore I will not enquire the Cause of this resolution, but – beleeve it is fitter for thee to Act, then mee to aske;

I have only this to demaund of thee, that thou wouldst not make me soe impoverishd by this graunt, that I have nothing els to –

331 *obedience*] cramped 340 *hath*] *th* heavily inked, perhaps altered 343 *call*] *Comaund* BSl

give to Basilino; accept of my first offer added to thy choyce; & leave me some request, even as a benefitt to ingage thee, by my p*er*formance of it to the like observance of my latest will: wch I shall wish noe other p*ro*secution of by Basilino, then such as the world shall find in me, of his imparted wishes in his absence;

Basil: I must againe in this removed extreame wish in silence to ~ – comprize an Answere, wch noe words can carry; you have bin Sr soe exact, in this yor blessing as you have put it into name, that it doth imp*ro*ve my obedience; you are now Sr soe enricht by this yor liberality, as I can aske you now a blessing, almost – equall to yor first, the p*ro*<.>ection of the heavenly ffidamira: in wch I dare boast some retribution of yor benefitts; having in her given you a subiect for the Exercise of all the worth & vertue that even you are king of; Then Sr yor leave to part im̄ediatly wth Agenor, only that I the sooner may begin to prayse the divinity of this yor goodnes;

King: Stay & but take these blessings wth thee; If it be fame hath prest thee, by giveing thee in hand already a share of publicke honour; may thy successefull daring carry thee soe soone to such a height of true renowne, that thou maiest quickly be somuch above the [<–––>] prayse of p*er*sonall Activenes, as even honor it selfe may soone restraine thee to com̄aund, & may send the hope to this I keepe but for thee, If it be love Attractivenes that drawes thee from vs, maiest thou obtaine vnknowne, wthout the helpe of any title showne; wch mayst thou give her in —

8.) reward.

reward, & not Condition, what er'e it be that parts vs Basilino, let [Fol. 6a] it be thy owne successe, not my distresse, that may bring vs soone to meete agine, for ffidamira you shall not be able to goe soe farr, nor soe conceal'd, but my strange care of her, shalbe tould you as the wonder of the time;

Basil: The Consciousnes vnto my selfe, of being your sonne is an ~//~ advantage, I am scrupilous of in any vndertaking; And I shall not soe distrust my selfe as to seeke more by my p*ro*fessing it; It is a title Sr I will leave here, & you shall not heare, you have a sonne abroad, but ⌜by⌝ my obedience to any of your sum̄ons, vpon

359 *into*] ~ *a* BSl 362 *pro<.>ection*] blotted, though the cross-stroke of *t* is visible 372] erasure damage covered with three pen flourishes; deleted word not decipherable, but barely visible ascender and descender suggest that it may have been *height*, by eyeslip from the line above 374 *hope*] *home* BSl *love*] *Loves* BSl 375 *wthout*] *out* cramped 379 *agine*] for *againe* 386 *by*] interlined with caret

wch I kisse these Royall hands;

King: ffarewell Agenor I looke to heare from you, what I expect from Basilino, 'tmay be vnfitt for him to write;

Agen: Best of Kings & ffathers remaine in Peace, till the loud gloryes of yor sonne, repay you these in teares of Ioy; *(Ex: Ba: Agen:*

King: Doe any of you know where ffidamira lives?

Tim: I doe S^{r}

King Goe then p^{r}sently & take some of the Guard wth you & bring her hither wthall hono^{r} & noe shew of violence;

Tim: I shall Sr *Exeunt.*

Scena: 5 ·
Fidamira: Agenor:

ffidam: 'Tis strange, this sudden resolution of the Prince! this is that he told me I should heare of, when he went a way: *(En: Agen:)*

Agen: The life of man p*ro*tracted to a miracle, were yet too short to tell the wonder of thy faith; much more that instant is but left me now for adoration of it; The Prince is instantly resolv'd to leave his ffathers [house] Kingdome, & hath obteynd his leave; & hath – chosen me the only p*ar*tner of his thoughts, & his Companion in his meant disguise; soe that heaven finding thy vertue such as – might easily be drawne into a miracle, resolves to raise it, vnto more Eminence, by this further tryall; And I, for this – their end am punish'd wth the love & trust of Basilino; The time wee had resolv'd for consu$\overline{m}$ation of our mutuall wishes; wee must now deferr, till our returne; sure ffidamira thou hast refin'de thy selfe to neare Divinity, thou art above the being enioyed by sence: & it were insolence in me to hope for such a tempta$\overline{con}$,

in

9)

in this absence as you have mett wth: but even the love is not soe impossible as my imbraceing it. The Princes parting doth depend on nothing now; but my returne, wch hee is ⌒– [FOL. 6b]

409 *punish'd*] ? apostrophe, perhaps touching up on loop of *d* through *y*'s descender *love*] ~ *of Queenes* FCos, BSt, BPet, 8°

410 *wishes;*] possibly a comma

414 *you*] pen stroke

416 *now;*] possibly a comma

almost as impatient of as I of staying here; wch is a ~//~ blessing I somuch repine to leave, as I have need of such an Angell even as you, to pray for my forgivenes of it;

ffidam: It is a strange resolve, Agenor; But sure heaven that had noe more to give him here, for a reward of his deserts, hath thus instructed him in the way of tasting all their blessings; his —– feeding for a while wth a pa*r*ticuler & Comon Pallate, that soe by Comparison (at wch wee must touch all our Ioyes to try how pure they are) hee might his more refin'd, There is a ~–– transcendency in that young man above his fate of Prince: & could any accident endeare Agenor vnto me, it should bee Basilino's trust, for the deferring of our wishes, the occasion is soe strange it doth import the will of heaven; And for the tryall of my faith, it is to easy & assur'd a thing for heaven – ti'ntend: if heaven meanes a miracle in mine, it must be by it's intirenes after the breach of yours: wch to me would seeme such a miracle, I should not wonder that my owne should be p^{r}serv'd for my affection; But this sad digression hath noe reason for it; but the distracted sence of your – departure; Goe then Agenor & serve that glorious Prince wth such successefull faith, that he may thinke at your returne (not knowing of our loves) by the opinion of thy faith, that nature meant our faiths only to match in one another: & for Improvement of our Ioyes wee — may have his share in the bestowing them: Stay not now for any thing, but for Confirmation of – my wish;

Agen: How opportune a blessing is the last Comaund of ffidam: by wch she doth appropriate my faith soe solely to her= =selfe, as she applyes my duty to the Prince, as meritorious vnto her: I can serve the Prince wth such a rare vnint^{r}ested faith, it shall not wish for recompence, having already more reward then he can give; the will of ffidamira: wch the Gods keepe for a reward of all his glorious deeds, at his returne, in giving her, but even somuch to give ffidamira:

10.) as

425 *might his*] *must find his* BSl; *might find his* FCos; not in BSt, BPet, 8° 431 *ti'ntend*] written as one word 434 *affection*] *affliction* FCos, BPet, BSt, 8° 444 *the*] *this* FCos, BSt, BPet, 8° 447 *vnint^{r}ested*] written as *vn int^{r}ested*; *ested* cramped 451 *her*] *him* FCos, BSt, BPet, 8°

[Fol. 7a]

as his consent vnto her will; wch (as the Consumation of his gloryes, & our Ioyes) I must expect, And now by loosing of our hands let fall this p*ar*tition, wch they yet hold vp; & in this darkenes pray our hearts may not lye long vnder this whole weight of love, they now must beare, but that our Eyes may be restor'd to ease them;

ffidam: Mine shall turne inward, all their light vpon my thoughts, wch shalbe soe pollisht, as they shall still answer to one another, wth the reflex of my Agenor's Image;
Move ffidamira now, & let's wth equall stepps fall thus from one another, while the earth wee tread, by interposing of it⌢ selfe betweene thy light & me, shall shadow out this darke⌢ Eclipse; *Exeunt.*

Scena: 6 ·
Basilino: Agenor:
Basilino in his Disguise.

I finde a yeilding in my *Genius* to the curiosity of – passing by the Shepheards paradice, in wch peacefull – harbour, I have heard of such a strange repaire of wrack't & hopeles fortunes as the distresse hath prov'd a blessing; ye institution of this solitary regality, wch they live vnder, – I have heard my father tell; & all their priviledg'd Lawes & Ceremonies; wch I have so well pleas'd to wonder at, as curiosity had once resolv'd me to satisfy it; by some disguis'd convenience, to the election of their Queene: wch is every yeare by the plurality of the sisters voyces; received into their order: wch is now neare this time *(Enter Agenor)*
Heere comes Agenor fitted for our Iorney; I'le advise wth him; you come Agenor opportunely to note in a case concernes you too; whether wee may fitly take this opportunity to see the Shepheards paradice, as wee passe forward to Navarre. 'Tis in our way as 'tis a Deviation into Noviltyes, wch guide sad

459 *they*] *t* corrected (? false start of long *s* for *shall* following) 461] speech heading *Agen:* missing 468–484] lines 468–477 have been justified to the nearer blind-ruled line, leaving the same margin width on both sides of the page; the lines then lengthen gradually until 484, which reaches the further blind-ruled line, to which all subsequent lines are justified 475 *it; by*] cross-stroke of *t* joined to loop of *b*; *;* inserted over joining stroke 480 *note*] *vote* FCos, BPet, 8°

thoughts, the best by a diversion of them out of their owne way; wee can have admission by a blanke of my ffathers, wch I can – produce; wth a p*ar*ticuler warrant for it, And the time of the election of their Queene (wch is every yeare the first of May) is now wthin 3· dayes: wch wee wth some Diligence may arive at; what say you Agenor? doth not this occasion move you too?//

I beleeve

11.)

Agen: I beleive it Sr a Curiosity worthy of an entire purpose ~ therefore not to be omitted, lying in the way of yor designes wch cannot be better begun, then by the information of yor selfe in such a rarity, as all forraigne Nations doe admire; for it is as it were an heavenly institucon, that extends its benefitts to all strangers, whose births are such as may be worth fortunes p*er*secution, & the distresses seeme soe desp*er*<.>te as may bring honour to the remedy; And this may prove Sr the neerest way vnto yor Iorneys end, the forgetting of ffidamira: for sure Beauty is soonest worne out of our – memory, by the imposicon of new weight vpon it, & soe the last prsseth away the former: And fame tells such ~~ wonders of the beauty of this place as sure it is rather – a religious feare, then yor fathers guard, secures their ⌢– solitude from invasion, on the prtence of Adoration, And it may be Sr the Gods will not indebt you, for so much as the – Composition of yor broken minde, to any Nation but your owne; [Fol. 7b]

Basil: Alas Agenor, do's't thou thinke that any Beauty, can er'e dis= =place the memory of ffidamira? why all Beauty and all – Excellence are [<~>] Coppyes of her; No, it must be a generall defacing of all her Sex, It must be Atheisme in love, not change of my Religion; It must be an vtter Abandoning of this my beleife, that beauty is but an Idea, not to be enioyed but by imagination, wch though the visibility doth seeme to – contradict & prove materiall, yet 'tis that, that makes it more delusive, not possible; for beauty & enioying are incompassible, & by this Atheisme, must I be sav'd Agenor;

493 *admire;*] possibly a comma 496 *fortunes*] *s* not well formed, joined distantly *desper<.>te*] blot obscures letter beneath 501 *former:*] possibly a semi-colon 510] paper damage covered by pen flourish suggests deletion, but no letters are visible 512 *Abandoning*] *A* heavily inked with cross-stroke otherwise used only in scribe's italic hand; surrounding paper damage indicates an alteration

Agen: There's nothing sure S^{r} soe impossible to be enioyed as your enioying this opinion long, vnles you could refine yor selfe into an Idea, abstracted from yor flesh: you not only loose yor memory, but all yor sences, to retaine this new opinion: can you thinke Sr Beauty was ne're enioy'd?

Basil: Never Agenor, There's no lovers soaring Phancy that won't – confesse the Beauty 'tis set vpon is even above his highest — thoughts; & soe endeare his thoughts, alleadgeth an impossibility of thinking high enough, can our sence then Agenor get vp to such a pitch, where even our Phancy flatts into excuse.//

12) *These.*

Agen: These are but lovers raptures that sometimes carry beauty above sence in any kinde, it were Iniustice to <.>equire of our sences the carrying vs above the ground, when they were not ordeyned to fly: their motion is toward fixt materiall obiects, wch they can reach & are not bound to comp^{r}hend lovers discriptions, that enlarge beauty into a spaciousnes, where it looseth itselfe, because it – cannot be compas't: Take this rule S^{r} sence is not bound to ⌢– follow any thing out of sight, & wthin those bounds, it can enioy all it meetes; [Fol. 8a]

Basil: Well Agenor, wee shall have leisure to discourse of this as wee goe; Lets set forward towards the Shepheards Paradice; wee must change our names; I'le call my selfe *Moromante*;

Agen: And I'le change my name into *Genorio*; wee must make hast S^{r} the Io^{r}neys equall the dayes wee have left for them; *Exeunt.*

Scena: 7 ·
King, Osorio: Timante.
ffidamira:

King: Are the Lodgings p^{r}par'd as I comaunded?

Tim They are S^{r} you are obey'd in all things;

King. When ffidamira comes bring her in; forbeare till then; I must doe her some honour, may be soe sudden, & soe strange, as may o're take Basilino, before he get out of our Kingdome;

525 *soe*] *to* BSl   529 <.>*equire*] initial *r* illegible because of smudged correction   548 *may*] cramped

Enter *ffidamira* all in blacke led by *Osorio & Timante* *The King lookes amazedly on her.*

King: I thought I might be attempted to owne some power, to oblige such a Creature in whome nature seemes to glory to have ~ ⌢ – bestowed all her's; yet I will not be soe vniust to the departed Basilino, as to appropriate any thing I am to deliver to you; for in his will, hee hath left you; all that I can give you; nor could I have beleev'd it could have been soe difficult, The – being Executor to a Prince: for I find more due to you, then he could bequeath, or I minister vnto you, Therefore vouchsafe (fayre mayd) to ease me somuch as to name yor wishes: since you have reduc'd a King to the beleife of having nothing ⌢ – worthy of you, & therefore dares not choose for you;

If.

13)

ffidam: If the departed Prince S^{r} hath in his will bequeath'd any – thing to pious vses, to purchase prayers for his successe and faire returne, yor Maiesty will prove a Provident dispencer of them in the choyce of me, whose devotion is already kindled in soe pure a flame as interest would dim it, & not nourish it, & even my wishes S^{r} are all soe cleere from any staine of selfe=advantage that they are such as your Maiesty cannot possesse me of; [Fol. 8b]

King: I will acknowledge ffidamira my impotency as a King in the – disposing any thing so worthy: & yet begg the knowledge of thy will in a more powerfull name, a servant vnto ffidamira, & by the vertue of that name beleeve my selfe enforc'd to a Capacity of any thing that she will wish;

ffidam: You have already S^{r} furnisht me wth an vnlook't for wish; — The expiation of this guilt, your prophanation of your selfe hath cast vpon me; I had another S^{r} soe innocent, as it were ⌢ fitt for you to ioyne in, thou you could not graunt; The Prince's ~ soone returne, soe Crown'd wth his desire, that he may thinke – hee brings more Ioy along wth him, then even your Crowne – – – can promise him: And this is S^{r} my only wish: & it is S^{r} soe ⌢ – propitious to me, as it makes your Ma^{ty} all the returne I can er'e

552 *attempted*] *tempted* FCos, BSt, BPet, 8° 565 *a Provident*] *an improvident* BSl 579 *thou*] for *though* *you*] blotted, perhaps false start *Prince's*] *n* has three minims 583 *er'e*] in margin

hope for these your offered benefitts, The wishing of you all increase of Ioyes & gloryes;

King: Doe not wonder ffidamira, at the title I tooke on me, I – speake to you in Basilino's name, & it was not improper in the p*er*formance of his will to vse his name; say 'twere himselfe, And I'me affraid I shall too soone take't vpon mee; The wish wch you have chosen hath soe farr indebted me vnto you as I must speake something now in my owne name, & retract the promise as I had made to Basilino; to possesse my selfe of all my power, wch I thinke yet too litle, to tempt thy modesty to the choyce of any thing it does conteyne, But doe not ffidamira in duty to yor King, reduce him to repine at his Condition, in havinge nothing to present you wth, but wishes back againe;

ffidam: In all humility & reverence to your power S^{r} I thus fall downe, to begg of you that (wch only as a King you may bestow) Liberty: wch I have chosen as the

14.) greatest

greatest blessing Kings are trusted wth: And I trust somuch [Fol. 9a] to your goodnes, that I thinke I need not bring the Gods for my dismission, whose Cause hath occasion'd this suite vnto – your Maiesty: The performance of some vowes wch will require privacy; And thus your Maiesty shall sett me att Liberty, that am (as yet) in bonds vnto my vowes;

King: You have made soe strange a choyce, ffidamira, as the ~ – vnwilling giving it endeares the guift, & that wch doth ~ – p*er*swade me most vnto this Graunt, is, that you shall take from me, that wch is dearer to me, then all you leave mee, your Company; And while you doe avoyd the meritt of my Actions; you cannot disapoint my sufferings of some desert vnto you: Therefore you shall choose what place agrees best wth your intent, If you will accept this Pallace, I'le leave it to you, And your privacy shalbe secur'd to you by a Guard that shall not come soe neere you, as to let you know you have any; Choose what Temple you like best, & the entrance shalbe forbid to all, but you: that noe impure breath may mixe wth yours; But ffidamira these your Devotions ~~– perfected, I shall expect you will accept our Court for ~//~

588–9 *say 'twere himself]* for stage direction; (*say to himselfe*) BSt

Sanctuary to that Saintlike Innocence, that shines about you;
It were impiety to let you live in the Crowd of Comon ~ –
persons; & your owne piety will enioyne you to allow my
Daughter your Company, as a patterne for vertuous youth;

ffidam: It would become S^{r} a retreat out of my selfe to be any ⌢–
where but in my ffathers house, whether I beseech you S^{r}
I may returne, & there remaine some few dayes; After wch
I shall obey your Maiesty wth that Devotion, wch is due to –
the Gods, whose Image you are; beleiving S^{r} you will comend
nothing but what [. .] ⌜shalbe⌝ meritorious to obey you in;

King: You shalbe ffidamira reconducted to you ffathers house
& there remaine vndisturb'd, till your owne leisure gives
mee admission to you; who wayts wthout? Carry backe ⌢ –
ffidamira to her ffathers howse;

How:

15)

Timan: How has this face displeas'd the King? that was resolv'd ~ – [Fol. 9b]
before he saw her to lodge her in the Pallace, wth such ~ –
prepared honours as rays'd all the Court into a wonder of –
the Cause; Me thinkes I finde more now then e're I could
have guest; *Exeunt.*

King alone.

King: Oh what a mock was this, to aske me liberty while she was
takeing me; I had not somuch power left as to keepe her here
when she would goe: shee is already Mistris of my will, soe as
she disposeth of it, even ag^{t} it selfe; whether shall I repaire
for Liberty, that am beseig'd by my owne Guard? These ⌢
trayterous Eyes I must condemne them to perpetuall ~ ⌢
darkenes, or they'le betray me to such another light as will
darken all my other sences, even by the inflamation of them;
will love be content wth no lesse Trophee, then the invertion
even of nature turning the branches downe into the ground
& making [<~~⌣ ⌣>] the rootes to budd & blossome in the aire?
Must love needs have a Garland of such prodigious ~ –

625 *become*] *be to me* FCos, BSt, BPet, 8° 630 *shalbe*] interlined with caret above heavy deletion 631 ²*you*] for *your* 651] erasure damage covered by four pen flourishes, no letters visible *aire?*] *;* altered to *?*, comma remaining under head of *?*

fflowers? Now *Basilino*, I finde thou hast left me some= what to doe for thee, worthy of a King to bragg off, the wrestling wth these passions for thy sake, wch els I should imbrace, & lett into my heart, as an inlargement of it, & my life;

But I will soe allay this heate,
By takeing thee into it's seate.
As that it still shalbe wth stood
As if I liv'd but by thy blood.

Exit.

The:

16.)

The song after the first Act: [FOL. 10a]

Victorious love though it hath gott the day.
Asham'd of such a Combat flyes away:
And now doth arme it selfe wth sacred fire
To goe securely from all wilde desire.
And innocence in this vnhappy strife,
Looseth her fortune, though she save her life,
You have beheld two lovers soe neare death,
By parting, as you may feare more their breath,
Can't last to bring them back to meete againe
Then meeting it should eithers vertue staine,
But the effects of Absence none can knowe.
But they that curs'd are to have knowne it soe;
Ambitious love wth nature oft contends.
And soe is often cros't as it ascends;
But in this contestation wee shall see
Them strive like th'elements; but to agree.

655 *for*] *f* very heavily inked, perhaps altered 656 *inlargement*] written as *in largement* 669 *fortune*] written as *for tune*

And soe they will not frustrate eithers vse
But somewhat of each other thus produce.

17.)

Actus Secundus.
Scena Prima [FOL. 10b]

The Scene removed to the
Shepheards Paradice:

(*Enter:* *Bellessa chosen Queene.*
Camæna: Pantamora:
Vortorio: Melidoro:
Mastiro: Moromante:
Genorio:

18.)

Act: 2 · Scene: 1 · [FOL. 11a]

Vot: The Gods Belessa by the voyce of your sisters have chosen you Queene, & you must now take your Throne, wth this oath I am to give you for the faire observance of all those Conditions, vpon wch, you are trusted wth this Crowne: wch are the faithfull⌢– –execution of the Lawes wee live vnder, & reigne over; *(Read the oath)*

Bell: Give me leave (faire sisters) while I am my selfe before I doe⌢— become your Creature (& soe more obliged) to wonder at your goodnes: & to renounce all meritt to this honour: vnles the being surprized by it, may passe for any; wch if my passion doe not prove enough, my forraigne birth, will certefy much more; wch

681] *1* and 7 of page number joined at head end stroke of preceding *e*   689 *Mastiro*] for *Martiro*   697 *(faire*] opening bracket inserted over

as it might advance me towards your tutelar Civilityes, must needs remove me from the p^{r}tention to this Eminence amongst you; Therefore your former favours can only give a reason for this excesse, that to recover the desperate debt I owed you all, you have resolv'd to lend me more, soe to enable me to make a retribution wch may comprize them all: And for this end I may avow a Ioy in this your Choyce; wch I shall study soe to iustefy your Iudgm^{ts} in, by the complying wth the obligations both of your debtor & your Queene, as when I shall resigne that name I shall have purchas'd one I shall esteeme as much, A *Creditor* to all of you;

Cam: Pant: Wee two Bellessa are deputed in the name of all, to assist at the Ceremony of your oath, & the publication of yor Lawes;

Voto: Proceede Bellessa to the reading of the oath;

Bell: sweares.
By Beauties Innocence & all that's faire.
I Bellessa as a Queene doe sweare.
To keepe the honour & the Regall due:
without exacting any thing that's new:
And to assume to me no more, then must
Give me the meanes & power to be iust;
And (but for Charity & mercies Cause)
Reserve noe power to suspend the Lawes;
This I vow even as I hope to rise
From this vnto an higher Paradice.

Voto: When your highnes hath possest your Throne,
I must begin to read the Lawes;

That. 19)

Bellessa ascends the Throne [FOL. 11b]
Votorio reades.

---

1. That a Queene is to be elected the first of May every yeare, by the plurality of the sisters voyces, from wch election the brothers are excluded;
2. That the Queene must be aged vnder Thirty, & beauty to be most regarded in the Election;
3. That both the brothers & sisters must vow Chastity & single life,

while they remaine in the order, & the breach of this Law is to be punish'd wth Death;

4. That every yeare at the Election of the Queene, what brother or sister shall desire to retire out of the Order, vpon designe of marriage, shall then (vpon their demaund) be lycenc'd, & at noe other time;

5. That the Queene shall admitt none [..to] into the order but one every yeare by grace, the rest vpon publication of their ⌢– prtence: wch must be either a vow of Chastity, (wch is not ever to be dispenc'd wth) or the verefication of some misfortune worthy the Charity of this honourable sanctu<.>ary; wch all the Brothers and sisters are to be Iudges of,

6. That all nations are to be admitted vpon iust prtences;

7. That there is noe propriety of any thing among the Society; but a Comunity of all wch the world calls riches or possessions;

8. That detraction from the honour of a sister, wthout proofe, is to be punish't wth the same penalty made for the faulty;

9. That noe brother or sister shall ever goe out of the lymitts of the kingdome but by a finall dismission;

10. That noe such shalbe receiv'd againe vpon any prtence;

11. That strangers shalbe admitted only by the grace of the ⌢–– Queene, or by p*ar*ticuler warrant from the king; & (vpon noe Condicons) shall stay above three dayes;

Voto: These are the Lawes your Maty is sworne to protect; And now I in the name of all the blessed society, bow in obedience to you:

Cam: Pant: Wee in the name of all the sisters, salute you Queene & begg to leave the seale of all our Dutyes, on your royall hands;

(They kisse her hand)

20.)

Now

Voto: Now, Madam after an howers rest, the order requires yor Maiestyes [FOL. 12a] repaire vnto the Temple, there to p*er*fect all the Ceremony;

Belles: I can have noe such rest, *Votorio*; as on my Knees before the Gods: for I have yet a greater blessing to implore of them, then this they ⌢ have bestow'd their propitiousnes towards my discharge of what – they have bestowed vpon me;

743 *[..to]*] ? *vnto*, deleted by heavy single line covering severe paper damage 747 *sanctu<.>ary*] blot 766 *Now,*] ? comma; perhaps a pen mark 771 *bestowed*] *imposed* BSl (by eyeslip from 770)

Princes Votorio have noe lesse:
To pay the Gods, then to possesse:

— Exit looking on *Moroman: Genor:*

What are these strangers?

Voto: They were admitted Madam by warrant from the king;

| *Moram*: *Geno*: stay *Votorio*.

Moram: If your Lycence S^r allow you soe welcome a civility as to satisfy a strangers curiosity, you may oblige vs, in acquainting vs, wth what the Queene said;

Voto: My profession S^r & your habit both enioyne me (after I have satisfyed you in this demaund) to offer you my service in easing you of any curiosity this place hath put vpon you; The Queene desir'd only to knowe whoe you were, & how admitted; wch I gave her an Account of as farr as my knowledge led me; wch was noe further then your – admission by the kings letters;

Mor: The lymittation S^r wch is vpon ⌜the say of⌝ strangers here; (where curiosity is fed, faster then it can swallow, much less digest) might excuse an – – importunate detention of any one, but you S^r whose habitt renders you S^r soe necessary to the residents, as it were a Sacriledge to ⌢ rob them of your time;

Voto: As it is a pious worke (the distribution of Hospitall Civility) I am the proper'st you could have mett S^r to pay the ingeniousnes of yor curiosity, wth the knowledge of any thing you can aske for;

Mor: Since this civility may be meritorious to you S^r I shall the willinger, put you to the exercise of it; And first I would gladly knowe the antiquity of this instituted regality; & the occasion of it; & the rest of the particulers of this place, wch my ignorance cannot furnish me wth questions for;

Voto: The Ingeniousnes of this institution is such as wee may Ioy, wee doe not owe it to Antiquity; it derives it selfe noe higher then ye kings Grandfathers time; who had a Daughter call'd *Sabina*, a – Lady of that strange Beauty & perfections as this was, but one of the miracles she left vs to admire her memory by;

The

21)

The vertue of her resolution takes of much from the wonder of [Fol. 12b]

784 *gave*] *ga* not well separated, *a* perhaps altered from *i* 787 *the say of*] interlined with caret, *a* inked twice *say*] *staie* BSl 796 *knowe*] *e* blotted, not well formed

her will, wch seemes to have remain'd imperious, & not flexible to her distresse; she was sought by two Princes, the Daulphine of ffraunce, & the Prince of Navarr; whose passions seem'd soe equall, as the most powerfull could not beare a Denyall, & the weaker thought himselfe soe arm'd by his passions, as he despis'd the anger wch the power of – ffraunce had vow'd ag^{t} him, if he were preferr'd; Sabina's inclination to Navarr, drew downe the mighty power of mighty ffraunce vpon this Prince: but the hope of faire Sabina (wch he seem'd to thinke him selfe a Gayner by, after the losse of most of his Countrey) ~ – animated him: Then Sabina, whome it seemes the love of vertue only had made partiall to Navarr, found the way to exalt her vertue more then by persisting ag^{t} difficultyes, wch seem'd to take of from the glory of it, by the abatem^{t} p*ro*cured where it intended an advantage: & soe fearing least his sufferings might rayse his vertue, to such an estimation, as he might be thought to have deserv'd her, (& soe the matching of herselfe might lessen her) resolv'd to take the – glory wholly wth the sufferings to herselfe: & soe sent to offer to the victorious Daulphine, (that had already made him selfe Prince of Navarr, & bragg'd that wth that title hee would wooe *Sabina*) her promise: That vpon Condition of his restoring Navarr vnto ye Prince, & swearing future Peace, she would never marry the Prince of Navarr; The Daulphine (whose successes had nourish't his love (even in Sabina's direct denyalls) wth hope) swallowed this as an assurance of his wish, wthout examining the words, but securely beleiving his owne flattering omen; And although Navarr ~//– refus'd the treaty & the future peace, yet he instantly p*er*form'd all that Sabina ask'd; who now resolv'd to publish the p*er*formance of her promise; she begg'd leave of her father to make a vow of Chastity, & desir'd the propriety of this place as her Dowry, wch nature seemes to have made of such an vnmatch't delightfulnes, as if she meant to have bragg'd that she had made a stage on earth worthy of Sabina's acting this her Divinest part vpon; Hither then, by the consent of her indulgent father *Sabina* came, attended by many nobles of both sexes, whom love to Sabina or admiration of the Action brought wth her: of wch she made this order; And, authoriz'd by her ffather, erected this royall governm^{t} & enacted all the Lawes you have heard read, wch

812 [1]*mighty*] not in FCos, BSt, BPet, 8° 818 *advantage*] *vantage* cramped 826 [2]*Prince*] cramped 840 [1]*of*] end of cross-stroke blotted

have byn soe inviolably kept, as a punishm^{t} here would - - seeme a wonder;

22.) *She.*

She enioyed the Regency during her life, & then left the p*ro*priety [FOL. 13a] of all vnto the Queene; wch is elegible as you have heard; The – peace & setlednes of this place is secur'd by natures Inclosure of it, on all sides by impregnablenes, as if it was meant for Chastity only to make a plantation here; at one passage only the Rockes ⌢ seeme to open themselves, wch is mainteyn'd by a Garrison of the kings, wch deliver all strangers to vs as sutors not Invadors; Thus have I inform'd you of the institution of this order, wch was call'd by the ffoundresse *The Shepheards Paradice*, as being a ~ ⌢ – peacefull [<~~~~⌣⌣>] receptacle of distressed mindes, & sanctuary ag^{t} fortunes severest executions: Now S^{r} I must needs tell you the generous end of the Prince of Navarr, that you may see there was nothing accessary to this heavenly institution, that had not a transcendant newnes of bravery; The Prince (as it seemes, ⌢ hating that earth, whose safety hath occasion'd his losse of Sabina) in scorne of it, forsooke it, & came hither in a disguise, & was ⌢ – admitted into the order; where he liv'd conceal'd, & dying wthout – ever making himselfe knowne to Sabina: but at his death left such a notorious memory: as all ages ages shall study to blazon it, & put it to the royallest Ornam^{ts} that can be due to Princes; The Queene ordain'd a p*ar*ticuler Ceremony to be p*er*form'd every yeare at this Tombe, wch is iustly observ'd;

Mor: This is soe heavenly a Tradition, as it becomes best yor delivery; This order seemes a match betweene love, honour & Chastity; wch you are happy S^{r} being the Preist to; but give me leave to wonder why the brothers are excluded out of the Election, wch is to bee guided most by beauty; of wch sure they are best Iudges;

Voto: The reason S^{r} that I have heard was then given by the ffoundresse; that it had bin to have made them Iudges in their owne Causes: – since there is noe man but hath a p*ar*ticuler interest that doth ~ – p^{r}possesse his choyce; whereas all women are rather Inquisitors, then Admirators one of another, & being voyd of passion noe ⌢ freindshipp, can incline them to yeild priority in beauty: & so 'twas

849 *to*] false start on *t*, perhaps of long *s* 851 *sutors*] pen slip at end of ^{2}*s* 854] erasure damage covered by five flourishes, no letters visible, first stroke lost of *r* of *receptacle* following *sanctuary*] ^{2}*a* touched up 856 *generous*] written as *gener ous* 863 *ages ages*] for *ages* 866 *this*] *his* BSl

thought most probable, & where most of them agreed to yeild, the advantage must be vnquestionable;

Mor: The wisdome S^{r} of the ffoundresse was such, as it carryes away our Admiration, even wth this our preiudice: I have one satisfaction – more to desire of you, wch the omission of, I doe beleive (in yor opinion) render me vnworthy of these I doe already owe: The knowledge of this your now Queenes Condition; & the time of her admission & her p^{r}tence;

'Tis

23.)

Voto: 'Tis not above a yeare since she was received, soe that had shee [FOL. 13b] not had, such a transcendant beauty as might have endur'd the ~ – abatement of what the envy of soe sudden an elevation, might have taken from her, & even [<~~>] after that deduction have remayn'de ⌢ incomparable, sure she had not bin chosen; 'Twas thought Pantamora the last Queene would have bin re=elected; She is by birth a stranger of some part of ffraunce, & brought wth her markes of noble birth; her p^{r}tention was an intention of her ffather, to dispose of her to a p*er*son of great worth & quality, who then lov'd another soe passionatly, as the contestation wth his ffather about his consent, was so loud, as the noyse of it came to this Ladyes eares; who mov'd (as she said then) wth the true hono^{r} of her sex, resolv'd rather (out of duty to her p*er*fections then pride of them) not to expose, them to such an — vnder valuation, as the dispute of being enioy'd; Therefore she left her ffathers house, & repaired to this Sanctuary for protection of her beauty, wch was in danger of this prophanation; This was - - [<~⌣ ⌣>] received by all as an acceptable plea for admission, as a ⌢– Triumph that beauty had gott by flying; she hath liv'd here ever since wth soe reserv'd a modesty, as it hath soe reconcil'd the plurality of the sisters to the strangenes of her birth & beauty as her choyce may be ascrib'd rather to an Inspiration from above, then her aspiring thither;

Mor: You may well ascribe it to the Gods S^{r}; Wee never mett a greater temptation to an incivill detention, then the pleasingnes of your conversation; therefore wonder not if wee cannot retire from you; wee have two dayes yet to stay, & wee shall wayt on you ⌢ before our retreat from hence;

889] erasure damage covered by two smudged flourishes, no letters visible 902] erasure damage covered by three horizontal strokes, no letters visible

Voto: There's nothing Sr but my publick duty could call me away from my attendance on you; It is a part of my function the enterteinmt of strangers; soe to secure the privacy of the Society;

Mor: Wee Sr shall not faile to addresse our selves vnto you to receive as much comfort at our departure, as sorrow will admitt of; wch — wilbe yor blessing;

Voto: Sr I must leave that wth you now; ∠ *Exit. Voto:*

Mor: What say you Genorio are not you indebted to this digression of my curiousity?

Take.

24)

Geno: Take not vpon you the direction Sr it was some infusion from [Fol. 14a] above; but doth your curiosity carry you further yet? doth not this place p*ro*mise you the diversion you seeke from thinkeing on ffidamira? Here you have your choice either of the remedy I have prscrib'd, or that wch you invented: The admission of new beauty to displace that; or you may harden your selfe by the ⌢ - neglect of this; into such an habitt of Insenciblnes, as you may be of proofe agt all temptation;

Mor: Had not my vow Genorio a much more noble ayme, then myne – owne ease, I might consent to let it fall here & breake, even to humour thee; soe litle I esteeme my selfe, but I have pointed it at the expiration of a guilt, that doth soe Darken me as the neglect of beauty might now seeme a Curse of blindnes on mee; But when I have cleer'd my selfe of that, then Genorio, I will returne even hither (if thou wilt) wth open Eyes, to let thee see my quarrell to my selfe is stronger then love can reconcile; in living soe vnmoov'd wth beauty as *ffidamira's* suit to me, should not vnsetle mee;

Geno: I can imagine noe Quarrell you ⌜can⌝ have to yorselfe but one wch this resolution of insencibleness of beauty must compose: The misfortune of the Princesse of Navarr, whose repaire you cannot tender soe much being voyd of the sence of beauty;

Mor: 'Tis that *Genorio* as shall set a value on my pennance, the prostitucon of my selfe to her only for pardon, not reward; I will seeke her only to add glory more vnto her; the forgiving me; & when I have but seene her, Il'e there my guilt, & take in place of it, the punishment

914 *a part*] distantly joined 921 *curiousity?*] head of *?* written above comma 922 *infusion*] written as *in fusion* 924 *thinkeing*] written as *thin keing* 928 *into*] corrected from *vnto*, *i* heavily inked 933 *expiration*] *expiation* BSl *Darken*] *D* heavily inked, altered from ? *t* 939 ²*can*] interlined with caret 941 *cannot*] final down-stroke of *a* run together with first minim of *n*

of never seeing her againe; Mee thinkes Genorio, had I but once paid my Devotion to her hand, I should then rest, absolv'd in peace;

Geno: Looke S^{r} how wee are blessed? The Queene comes this way, & the Preist leading her. – Let's stand by. *Enter Queene wth her Trayne towards the Temple.*

Voto: Madam these strangers Curiosityes assure me they would bee – displeas'd to leave any priviledge vnenioyed, if yor Ma^{ty} shall vouchsafe them this hono^{r} of your hand to their welcome here;

Queen: What Countrey men are they?

Voto: Castilians Madam: *Moram: Geno: Kisse her hand.*

Queen: This place is civill, only in makeing all nations equally strangers, that are not residents; if they be not soe to vertue, & honour: *Exit.*

I am 25)

Gen: I am not yet soe fast but I can fly, & that only to p^{r}serve my faith [FOL. 14b] & Liberty; while I intended to keepe the Prince here as neerer ffidamira; I finde my selfe removing from her; Come S^{r} we have seene all shall wee goe on in pursuite of your designe?

Mor: Oh what Inchantment's this? methinkes I finde my selfe fixed – here; & yet the vertue of this touch, quickens, & moves my sences, soe as it implyes Divinity, rather then Magicke; me thinkes I finde the hand that holds me as it p^{r}sseth, print Characters vpon me such as my heart reades and is satisfyed for this detention

Geno: In what Contemplation are you S$^{r?}$ will you set forward toward yor lodging to p^{r}pare for yor Iourney?

Mor: I was thinking *Genorio* how ridiculous a thing yor proposition – of staying here was; since if wee would, the order admitts it not;

Geno: It were great losse of time in yor designe;

Mor: How might wee conceale, or disguise our selves if wee meant it?

Geno: The meanes were not soe vnfitt, as the resolution: for the way must be noble, by a direct p*ro*fession of some misfortune, & soe be receiv'd into the order: wch the vndisguising of your selfe, would dispence wth; but S^{r} let's goe it growes late;

Mor: Wee cannot goe before wee be dismist by the Preist, whoe is now assisting at the publicke service; wee must wayte the Queenes

946 *I'le*] *leaue* BSl 968 *S$^{r?}$*] head of $^{?}$ joined to head of *r* 979 *dismist*] ^{2}*i* joined to *s* at top of *i*; if not dotted, would more closely resemble *c*

returne from the Temple, & soe take our leaves of him; That (aside) hand wth one touch more, would plant me here;

Geno: I doe not like this backwardnes S^{r} sure the Princesse of *Navarr* is not here; I am ioy'd to find the burthen of your guilt soe to – lighten, as you doe rather choose to stand still vnder it, then – move towards your discharge of it;

Mor: I am soe willing to be punisht for her sake Genorio, as I take kindly this reproach; And as you are her Sollicitor, be also my guide towards her, & tell me, where you thinke the — likelyest place to finde her, for in Navarr, wee may beleeve she cannot be, soe long conceal'd from her ffather;

Enter *Queene* & Company from the Temple, & meete them as they goe out

Geno: Wee must now needs stay while the Queene be past;

26.) I vnderstand

Queen: I vnderstand you are Castilians Gent: came you lately from – the Court? [FOL. 15a]

Mor: Wee come directly from thence Madam, & made such hast to be here at the Ceremony [<~~>] of the Election, as it is but three dayes since wee left the king;

Queen: How doth the King, & Prince? have any of you had such accesse to the Prince as to be able to enforme vs of his p*er*son & his hono^{r}?

Geno: The honour Madam I have of being his Domestique, allowes me to thinke my selfe a fitter reporter of [<~~>] him, then this Gentleman: for his person Madam, nature hath throwne away many p*er*fections on it, wch his birth needed not to make him lovely; for the ~⌢– Composition of his minde it seemes to have byn iniur'd by his birth, that exposes him to somuch probability of flattery; the ⌢ - truth of his vertues being such, that Parasites deceive themselves in the exaltation of them; In my opinion Madam, he hath all that youth can bragg of, & all that age can reproach youth wth the – want off;

Queene. I have heard the Prince much valued by all relations, & also of a strange passion of his for a Lady of his Court;

Geno: 'Tis true Madam, hee hath long lov'd a Lady called *ffidamira*, which

995] *6* of page number *26* inked twice
999] erasure damage covered by two smudged flourishes, no letters visible
1003 *Domestique*] *D* heavily inked, smudged
1004] erasure damage covered by two smudged flourishes

is such a Subiect for a noble passion, as even the Princes Constancy seemes noe wonder: the only strangenes is that she is not mov'd towards him by his vertues; not that hee moves not from her, by her neglect;

Queene You give her Beauty a great power, that can dispence wth her – discretion, & the obligation to her Prince; Did you ever see her S^{r}? for I p*er*ceive your freind is p*ar*tiall to her.

Mor: I have Madam & doe allow her all the Beauty in this world that's left out of this Society;

Queene Wee are not subiect S^{r} soe early to envy, that you should neede to qualify so soone yor freinds prayses of her: But pray ye S^{r} wth the Prince persist in this meritorious constancy?

Geno: There was a Report Madam when wee came from Court that the Prince (to Crowne her vertue & his wishes) had offered her marriage, wch she excused the acceptation of by a præ=ingagem^{t} of her ffaith: & that the generous Prince resolving to dye wth her, for the braver fame took this excuse, wth the humility of a private servant, & resolv'd to leave his ffathers Court, that at some distance from

her

27)

[FOL. 15b]

her, he might setle his resolution of leaving her, her liberty & takeing his againe;

Mor: This wee heard Madam, but dare not affirme it as true;

Queene ffame of it selfe charg'd wth the weightyest things, is light enough to be suspected: but carrying lovers Quarrells it growes incredible, for thoughts cannot reconcile them, And soe the truth wch fame setts out wth may be chang'd before it can arive; If this were true (though it be hard to decide an advantageous glory, in this case to – either of them) yet I should incline to recompence the Princes sufferings wth some odds of honour, since she is to enioy her wish & he nothing but the vertue of p^{r}ferring hers: what say you Ladyes?

Pant: It is a strange vertue Madam, wch must p^{r}serve faith soe ⌒ – entire, when it may be set in a Crowne: I confes I wonder more at her, that might have had soe large an envasion as a Kingdome;

Cam: I beleeve Madam, the Prince's vertue hath resisted by farr the – greater Temptation: for her Insenciblenes might haue iustefyed his

1022 *to her.*] *t* corrected, heavily inked, *o* very small, *her.* cramped   1025 *early*] *easily* FCos, BSt, BPet, 8°   1026 *wth*] *doth* BSl   1031 *dye*] *weye* BSl; *vye* FCos, BSt, 8°; *vey* BPet   1039 *thoughts*] ^{1}*h* and *g* slightly blotted   *cannot*] *o* blotted   1044 *Ladyes?*] cramped   1047 *envasion*] *evasion* BSl

charge, but even his constancy could not authorize her: ffaith — must be sett wthout a foyle, soe every blemish wilbe visible; should a Prince scratch or deface a Iewell while he kept it in his owne hands, he might set what price he would vpon it: but in the – – Com̄on estimation, that would deprize it; soe must ffidamira have lost of her true value, though the Prince had rated her as high as ever; soe that she seemes to have preserv'd her value, & the Prince (for her sake) to have vndervalued himselfe: wherefore I should repaire him by allowing him the greater share of glory;

Queene. Whensoever you see the Prince againe, you may let him knowe how his hono^{r} hath byn noted here, & prevayl'd against the Competition of our owne sex;

They are goeing out

Mor: Give me leave Madam to receive our dismission by your – royall hand, & to wish the Prince had but once seene your — Maiesty: The desperatnes of the ill, & the Eminence of the – afflicted both concurr to make the cure worthy of you;

Queene. I could wish S^{r} hee did enioy the best p*ar*t of me, wch is the peace & quiet of my minde;

Exeunt.

manet *Mor: & Genor:*

Oh.

28.)

Mor: Oh what a blessed Creature's this! when even her wishes wch shee [FOL. 16a] thinkes most improbable, are in her power; & how condemn'd am I, that her wishing me ease, should prove a Torment to me: my ⌢ guilt's noe more a paine now, all I feele is this of leaving her;

Geno: My feare was quicker sighted then my sence, that Did propose to me at first the readyest safety that passion knowes, flying from Danger; wch I obey'd soe fast as nothing could have overtaken me; therefore my curse was faine to meete me, soe to bring me backe: & now methinkes I am soe fixed that I cannot move against my feare, for having bin soe bold as to precede my Love: Oh how - I curse my feare, for having disputed ag^{t} the Prin<.>e's staying here: But since my soule is charg'd I must disguise my selfe - also to the Prince: will you goe S^{r}?

Mor: How out of tune are these words, Genorio.

Geno: Have my words soe soone infected my voyce wth treachery that it

1050 *charge*] *change* BSl *her*] *hers* FCos, BSt, BPet, 8° 1056 *Prince*] cramped 1077 *backe*] final down-stroke of *k* thickened with heavy ink, almost obscuring following *e* 1080 *Prin<.>e's*] blot makes *c* indecipherable

betrayes me to the Prince! is't not the sence S^{r}? & not the sound that's out of Tune?

Mor: No Genorio, but me thought thy words were dragg'd along with such a sound, as if they had gone to suffer for some fault;

Geno: Alas S^{r} what Accent can fall low enough, to reach the Depth of our misfortune? no tune, nor words can sad enough the pitty that I owe you S^{r} that are not only going out of Paradice, but into such a Laborinth, as 'tis vncerteine whether every step carry you ~//⌒ backward or forward toward your end, since wee know not where to finde her;

Mor: 'Tis true Genorio, but how may wee vnwinde this maze of pilgrimage, & take the directest way vnto my vow?

Geno: Alas S^{r} 'tis a Case of Conscience, wherein I may better be a — Clyent then a Councellor; sure s^{r} the heavens that have infus'd this tender scruple of your guilt, will affect your Innocence somuch as to inspire your heart wth the directest meanes of expiation: for did they not intend you an vnblemish'd purity, they would ne're have mov'd you wth soe precise a tendernes, as even to me seemes superstition;

Mor: 'Tis soe iust a zeale that carryes me Genorio as the p*er*plexity of the way to it doth not distract my purpose: But heaven is soe ~⌒ – mercifull to my willingnes, as it presents me wth some meanes of

ease,

29)

ease, & offers me a lyne to guide my staying motions by: which [FOL. 16b] benefitt I count received, because I doe avoyd it for Genorio's sake;

Genor: Were it a discharge to you S^{r} to have me become as miserable as the reservation of your selfe from me, would make me, I should wth silence accept this Curse: But I beleive it must be an Assumption of more guilt vnto you S^{r} then yet you have: The – [<~~~~~>] suspition of my forwardnes & ability to ease you; But S^{r} nothing can seeme soe hard for me to act, as it is now to suffer this tendernes of yo^{rs} ag^{t} yor selfe;

1085 *Prince!*] head of *!* written above comma; head thick and heavily inked, perhaps an alteration 1095 *pilgrimage*] *rimage* cramped 1097 *Alas*] *A* heavily inked 1099 *somuch*] ? *so much*; joined distantly 1101 *vnblemish'd*] written as *vn blemish'd* 1107 *staying*] *straying* BSl 1114] five flourishes cover erasure, which has caused small holes in the paper

Therefore S^{r} let me begg it as a favour, your disposall of mee, as your opinion shall direct you for yor ease;

Moro: You may well begg this Genorio, for 'tis a suit will make you somuch richer then I, that I can ner'e discharge [,] my selfe of my indebtment to you; Therefore *Genorio* be not soe ambitious to pursue your suite;

Geno: What an amazing goodnes S^{r} is this of yo^{rs}? whoe know all the obedience the prostitution of this life could render you is soe much your due, as it could scarce Challenge prayse in easing you; you have plac'd me soe neare yor selfe, you have forgott what I was; you know s^{r} you have made me soe happy that I must trust to others to be sure, that I was ever miserable; give me leave s^{r} to accuse you [<~>] of forgetting me, when you would seeme to bribe my bloud to your [<~~~>] obedience, wth soe immense a treasure as obligeing you, whereas I should be overpaid wth yor acceptance of i'ts effusion, for your ease; Therefore S^{r} vnles you meane this as a Torment to me you must impart your thoughts;

Mor: How exactly kinde art thou Genorio; that wilt convince me by my love to the, not to my selfe: interesting thy ease in this my opening my thoughts;
I was thinking on the difficultyes of the way towards the directest end of this my Iourney; my Devotion to the Princesse of Navarr, & how the Information of thy selfe of her retiring & the most probable place of her concealment, might take off from me the laborious p*ar*t of search: affording me thease

30)

of

[FOL. 17a]

of staying here till thou cam'st backe to guide me: These were my thoughts Genorio; & would not such a debt, pawne me beyond redemption to thee?

Geno: I confes s^{r} you have found a paine, disputes the Ioy of easing you; wch nothing but the sence of leaving you, durst have ~ attempted; & this begining is soe hard, all that will follow will seeme done, this difficulty past;

Moro: Did not the perplexednes of the Inquiry leave thy successe —

1120 *discharge* [,] *my*] comma following *discharge* has been deleted by unusually lengthened first stroke of *m*   1129] erasure damage covered by single blotted line   1130] severe erasure damage, including small holes, has resulted in the possible disappearance of a final covering stroke or flourish   *immense a*] cramped   1133 *me*] pen mark under *e* could be comma   1136 *the*] *e* blotted   1139 *Princesse*] cramped, *i* not well formed   1140 *Information*] written as *In formation*   1142 *thease*] for *th'ease*

vncerteine, & assure thy paines; I might perswade away thy first obiection, since I must share the halfe of the first – paine of leaving;

Geno: Could I leave you S^{r} after that I could doe any thing? were she soe strayed from Mortalls, as destiny knew not where to —– finde her, my genius would direct me where to bring newes of her;

Moro: Alas Genorio the first paine of this our parting hath almost ⌢⌢ distracted thee: I will venture noe farther on thy temper: — since wee are both engag'd in this wilde Laborinth, wee will keepe together, that so though wee finde nothing, wee may not loose one another;

Geno: Stay S^{r} heaven is soe carefull of your ease, as it vouchsafes me (I thinke) even an inspiration that whispers to me that your staying here wilbe auspitious to you: soe that the Gods are pleas'd to recompence my losse wth a provision of your happynes; & now my leaving you, is become their direction; & the presage, of it, is made A Ioy; Therefore now I doe expect nothing but your instructions for my parting;

Moro: The Gods had neede ioyne wth me Genorio to recompence thy ⌢ meritt, I was resolv'd to stay here, & professe my selfe of the society, till you had found the way to this stray'd Saint; Then vpon your returne my profession of my selfe would – dispence wth this ingagem^{t}: & I might (guided by you) the easyer p*er*forme my vow;

Geno: I will goe S^{r} wthout expecting any meritt for my diligence, besides this of my obedience; for my minde gives me that your resting here, (not your remove) must setle you in peace; /

Come.

31

Moro: Come Genorio wee'le goe together to the Preist, you for dismission [FOL. 17b] I, for enterteinm^{t} //

Geno: I'le leave you S^{r} wth this presage that I shall find your Atheisme converted to Idolatry at my returne;

Mor: Me thinkes I finde my selfe nearer a ⌜change of⌝ Torment, then an ease;

Exeunt.

1159 *thee*] *th* blotted, *t* inked twice 1170 *to*] false start on *t*, down-stroke inked twice with curved ascender 1176 *diligence*] ^{1}*i* blotted 1179 *Genorio wee'le*] unusually long first stroke of *w* joins base of ^{2}*o* 1181 *Atheisme*] cramped 1183 *change of*] interlined with caret Fol. 17b] ink marks in lower left corner suggest the scribe was trying to get his nib working

Scena: 5 ·
Fidamira.

ffidam: Oh when doth Innocence reside? is she alwayes in her Iourney here on earth? & lodgeth but in Court sometimes? And that wch honour glory & ambition made their Iourneys end, The Pallace of Princes, she takes but in her way & presses on; is shee soe froward as not to love good Company? sure 'tis not that shee wants that pliable complacency wch is required in the society of Courts: she can't consent to give her selfe away in ~//– Complement, sure if she be fixed any where on earth, 'tis in the shade of solitude: where the cleere soule by the reflex of speculation shewes faire Innocence herselfe: where she enamour'd on her owne beauty lives, & makes selfe love soe meritorious, as it were sinne to be diverted from it; Thither must I carry mine, while it is yet vnstain'd. The breath of the Court would mist it over at last; should I consent to this intention of the kings, of placing me at Court though – it were wth a p^{r}tence of a Companion of his Daughter; why should he come hither to retract his p*ro*mise of my – privacy, before the time he had allowed it was expired? & he spake wth such a degradation of himselfe, as if he meant to aske me somewhat; which would not sute wth the — Divine Image; And therefore did depose himselfe from being a King, to make himselfe all man for his pretention; such preposterous humility to me could imply noe lesse though yet his words have had noe other guilt but theire – – submission; And I am bound in sence of all his gracious

care

32.

care, to provide ag^{t} the perversion of all this into sinne, & [FOL. 18a] to secure his Innocence even to my hazard; Therefore I must suddenly from home; And heaven to encourage me in this intent p^{r}sents me wth such a retreat, as may make the extremity a blessing: the Shepheards *Paradice*, thither will I fly: ffortune in [k] all her oppressions hath enrich't me, wth

1187 *when*] *where* BSl   1204 *expired?*] head of *?* written above comma   1206 *not*] false start; long *s* altered to form unusually long first stroke of *n*   1212 *sinne*] with only four minims   1217 *[k]*] incomplete *k* deleted with single stroke

a full p^{r}tence of my admission there; The Princes returne cannot aske lesse then a yeare: then shall I be free againe for my Agenor: whome (since this face hath now endanger'd in the losse of me) I'le change it till I may deliver it to him, Therefore it shall put on mourning, for it's faults & his -- absence: This order admitts equally of all nations, & as a Moore I will fly thither;

Love, let not this Averse disguise
Those of thy order scandalize.
Thy order's not advanc'd by beauty
So much as by a true loves Duty.

Exit

Scen: 6 ·
Bellessa: Martiro:

Mart: If this be true Madam of the Prince, he is some way happy, to have soe iust a p^{r}tence for your pitty.

Bell: Nay Martyro, that may inflict soe equivalent a pennance on him as may prove an abatem^{t} of that neglect, I was once bound to expresse, & I may love him then;

Mart: Are you soe well natur'd Madam as to apply Capitall punishments to the satisfaction of your Iniuryes? or may his sufferings ⌢ - reconcile him to your generous heart?

Bell: When he thought himselfe Martyro soe highly happy as he esteem'de the avoyding me, as a good fortune; that was a Condicon worthy of my scorne; wch then I did not in affectation of revenge, but of - right vnto my selfe, & now in this deiection, the same wish would p*er*swade me to restore him to his happines were it in my power, ⌢ wthout shaming him wth the knowledge of the author of it;

Did.

33

Mart: Did not I Madam somuch admire your transcendant vertues, [FOL. 18b] I should wonder at those Triumphs, the Gods have rays'd them too;

1228 *a*] blotted, with some paper discoloration 1240 *he esteem'de*] written as one word 1246 *Madam*] *M* altered from *m*

how well are the Princes Corrections, and your gloryes fitted? He,
by his fault to you is suspended from his principality in the –
Top of all his promis'd Ioyes, & you from your discontents are —
advanc'd the sooner to a Crowne;

Bell: 'Tis true Martiro, but the peace of my minde was never yet –
since I came here soe busy as to thinke any reputation due
to me; I have but an indifferent sence of this Crowne;
wch, as it is but Temporary, sits soe easy on me, I shall
not feele it, when 'tis taken off; I shall make vp the diminution
of my power of doing good, wth the addition to my time;

Mart: Give me leave Madam, to whome time's a burden to aske how
an addition to it, may prove an ease: you cannot better improve
this time then in such a Charity;

Bell: You must measure time Martiro, wth your soule, not yor sence:
you must not Antedate your desires soe as [<–>] time may seeme
too slow to bring you them: your wishes must not seeme to runn
a match wth times Quicke=sands: as they runne, their number &
their motion must be lesse; your Computation must be like
to that of Clockes, wch weigh & measure time at once, & nothing
lightens tyme, somuch as weighing it, If you must needs
wish something wthout yor selfe, let it be somewhat you —
may hope for; nothing takes more from time, then that;

Mart: Alas Madam I am soe free from this light variety of
wishes as I have but one, & that's so heavy, as it cloggs
times motion, & soe lengthens my dayes vnto me for a – –
tedious curse; & you have nam'd a remedy to refine my
torment, by the impossibility of my attayning it, Hope; —
for I am soe desperate I would not thanke my wishes for
any thing that I could hope;

Bell: This is then Martiro, a vanity in yor sufferings, not a desire of ease,
& pitty were a p^{r}iudice to you, as it would lessen the meritt of your
patience.

It were

34.

Mart: It were a Cheapning of your pitty Madam, to have it fall soe [FOL. 19a]
lowe, as my Condition; Princes can expect noe more from
you;

1257 *time;*] possibly a comma; line of text slopes sharply down from ^{2}*d* of *addition*, leaving point and comma of semi-colon widely separated 1262 *Antedate*] *t* heavily inked to correct an indecipherable letter beneath 1262] erasure damage covered by single line 1274 *impossibility*] *ssibili* slightly blotted, perhaps owing to hair on nib 1275 *thanke*] *change* BSl 1277 *ease*] cramped

Bell: The discent of pitty, Martiro, is the exaltation of it, love indeed should have an obiect levell to it selfe;

Mart: You could love then Madam, if you met wth an obiect Levell to your selfe: so as you might not seeme to incline to it but to – receive a Paralell;

Bell: I would not have the reservation of myselfe censur'd a defect Martiro, but an Election; I could love but vpon such termes, as – should reproach mankind wth a scarcity of meritt if I did not; & not taxe me wth a naturall repugnancy to love;

Mart: Vpon these termes Madam, you are equally iust to all our Sex, in this generall exclusion, by the Condicon of deserving you; for to that great disparity, all worth may seeme but equally distant, as all numbers are equally disproportionable to Infinity; ~⌒ Therefore Madam persist in this right vnto your selfe, & you – shalbe an vniversall wonder, not a private Ioy;

Bell: I feare not Martiro, as I doe not thinke my selfe worthy of a miracle made for me a purpose, (wch such a man must be as I could love) soe I doe not thinke the Gods will soe decline my thoughts, as to make me love lesse, then what I have propos'de them;

Mart: These thoughts are worthy of you Madam, love them still; soe – that your vertue may contest wth your person, whether nature or you have made the greater miracle;

Enter Votorio

Voto: The occasion Madam will aske pardon for this Intrusion on your Maiestyes privacyes; one of the Gentlemen that your Maiesty lately dismiss'd, demaunds admission into the Society & that your Ma^{ty} would appoint the time of his pretence; The other is departed.

Bell: I will deferr his wish a day; This afternoone give order for a – – Convocation: & I will goe & p^{r}pare myselfe for the Ceremony. *(Exit: Voto:) And 35·)*

Mart: And I will aske pardon of my love for all my past Complaints: [FOL. 19b] & bring my Ioyes in suffering to plead for a forgivenes; Hee – that will have the glory of a love, that out of choyce affects —

1296 *Therefore*] blot on cross-stroke of *f*   1297 *a*] false start from *t*, ascender remaining

impossibilityes, must needs delight in suffering; I will — p^{r}serve my voyce, & this darkenes shall keepe my passion from becomeing madnes;

Scen: 7 ·
Melidoro: Camæna:

Mel: Are you behinde Martiro, wee shall be stronger in our — excuse, The Queene is past they say to'th Convocation;

Mart: It is a faire excuse Melidoro for you twoe, yor being ⌢ — together: it will not seeme strange that the time escap'd you vnawarres: My being wth you may discredit your - - p^{r}tence, & imply you could not be soe pleas'd wth it as to forget how the time passed;

Cam: Noe Martiro, you must goe wth vs, exercise of Charity may better excuse a fault, then an idle pleasednes; wee may be thought to have borrowed the time, to lend your sorrow - some comfort: That's better then to have forgott it in our owne security;

Mart: I am not yet soe miserable, as to be releivable by soe cheape a Comfort, as Com̄on Charity; There is but one in the world happy enough to pitty me, & I can pitty all the world: whose Ioyes though they be cleere & make some noyse as they goe on, yet are soe shallow that the bottom's to be seene;

Cam: Come Martiro, this Cloud of yours may breake one day, then wee shall see what it conteynes;

Scen: 8 ·
Enter: Bellessa: Pant: Camæ.
Melido: Voto: Moram:

Voto: When your Ma^{ty} is plac'd the p^{r}tender (by yor leave) may begin his plea; *Queene Beginne.*

36 *Wth all*

1327 *pleas'd*] ascender of *d* heavily inked 1342 *Enter*] *r* unattached, and with short horizontal stroke to the right from base 1345 *Queene Beginne*] for speech heading *Queene*, speech *Beginne*

[FOL. 20a]

Mor: With all reverence to the presiding Ma^{ty} honour to the — blessed Society; Thus I lay downe my misfortune at your – feete; wch I finde I put off as I take new vpon me here: & I begin to grow doubtfull [<⌣⌣>] of the iustnes of my p^{r}tence; by a surprize of happines; wch enters soe fast by my Eyes, y^{t} I must fly back to my memory in hast, to bring out my — sorrowes; for I have such a new vnluckynes, made a purpose for me, as I ought to feare that this Ioy breakes in vpon me, to carry but away my memory, & wth it my p^{r}tence to this divine releife, & soe to make this instant lightning a ~ ~ perpetuall storme; Now I must first addresse my selfe to mine owne sex for Iudgm^{t} in what you Ladyes cannot be – – vmpires for want of experience in it, *loving against scorne:* I lov'd somuch I could have wish'd that even her scorne had bin preferr'd before any wishes, in this contynuance of my — passion, wch was soe vnhappy as to afford me many services done to her, wch I will not [<~~~>] expect somuch [.] reward for as their repetition: at last fortune made one day my life (wch was soe contemptible to me) the deliverer of hers & the p^{r}senter of what punishm^{t} she should appoint the barbarous attempter, whose threats, had almost sav'd the ⌢ — active guilt of spilling of her bloud, by that cold examination feare had drawne over her: wch notwthstanding did her that service as to send forth some faint cryes, wch guided me to the rescue in a wood whither my dispayre had carryed me to envy the life of plants, & to dispise my owne; There I found her on her knees, p^{r}pared to be a sacrifice to that – blow was moving towards her, when I came in to intercept it, guilt is soe weake as 'tis noe vanity to say I easily ~//– became asmuch master of his life as he was of hers; & offered her to purge the grownd that had borne such a – monster wth his bloud, she then I may say properly comeing to herselfe seemed to begg of me wth more curious ~ ⌢ earnestnes his life, then she had done her owne of him, as if her soule had byn already carryed vpp to heaven;

1349] erasure damage covered by two lines, no letters visible 1360 *any*] *my* BSl 1362] erasure damage covered by three lines, no letters visible 1362 *[.]*] single letter deleted by thick line; beginning of long down-stroke, perhaps false start of preceding *somuch* or following *for* 1366 *threats,*] comma perhaps an accidental pen mark 1368 *her:*] slightly blotted from erasure on verso 1375 *hers*] ? *her's*; vertical pen mark at tail of descender of *y* above (*easily*) might be an apostrophe

and

37

[FOL. 20b]

& owed him this fright for a blessing, I disarming him — only, obliged her: & gave him not only his life, but more — then mine owne: for when he was gone, she told me shee forgave him, since he had free'd her from an Iniustice; & that her life was only welcome to her, to retract her ⌢ — neglect of me, wch she would recant as farr as faith & hono^{r} would warrant her: I was impatient to knowe how farr these lymittations did extend, whither my ⌢ wishes were shutt out by them or noe, she told me the execution I had staid, was vpon a Condemnation where I had byn produc'd as a witnes against her: And that the p*er*son that I saw ready to be the Executioner; was one she lov'd soe well as she begg'd this a blessing of him: The – dying first; soe to end wth a perfect innocence; since his Iealousy had resolv'd the death of both, & that she had soe much dispaire of this request, as that had given me time to be the suspender of this Iudgment; Therefore that I should not wonder if she were tender of his life, for shee could not have liv'd after him, but must have dyed wth the guilt of her owne hands:, wthall she told me that it was of me only he was iealous; & therefore bad me weigh the meritt of my Actions, wth the vnhappines of my being the occasion; I wondred [<—>] to finde my selfe indebted to her, even after such a present as twoe such lives were vnto her; Therefore acknowledging my misfortune — (sacrificeing this releife of her to chance) I beg'd of her som coma̅und, whose p*er*forme might absolve me from the fault of my Contribution to her distresse, wth p*ro*mise to vndergoe whatsoever she should promise, a full ~//~⌢ forgivenes on:, Then she wth asmuch security as ⌢ — rigour, condemn'd me to more then I had freed her – from: & told me that this mistake of her intended — Executioner, did not somuch as abate her passion to him; & could much lesse dispence wth the'ngagem^{t} of her faith to him:

1381 *blessing,*] perhaps *;* 1384 *an*] head of *a* not well formed; perhaps a false start 1385 *was*] short vertical pen stroke downwards from head of *s* 1393 *this*] ~ *as* BSl 1394 *since his*] paper damage between the words 1403] thick black line over erasure damage 1414 *the'ngagem^{t}*] written as one word

[Fol. 21a]

Therefore she coma̅u̅nded me never to see her more, & to rest contented all my life wth the Ioy of haveing made her happy; After this hard Coma̅u̅nd she steept it (to⁀soften it) in much teares, as I grew rather asham'd then vnresolv'd; Then she began to praise & magnify the – bravery of this my Action, soe that I was afrayd to heare her long, least vanity should seeme to share wth her, in the perswasion of this Action, I gave her instantly my p*ro*mise of complying wth her will; & to add somewhat even to her owne wish, I said I would conduct her to her owne servant, & never more, but once againe to him, accuse her of her Cruelty: and would ioy that my accusation of her, might now prove meritorious to her, And to setle her in Peace, and confidence wth him, I would make him witnes of my vow soe to secure her future Ioyes; This I did the same day, & soe left her, iust where she began to be sensible of my Company: & resolv'd to repaire to this Sanctuary, wth soe much forgetfulnes to devotion, as nothing, but the hope of my admission here could have p*er*swaded me to the repetition of this story; wch if it doe p*ro*cure me, I may triumph over fortune, whose depression of me hath but suncke me to the Center of rest & peace. //

Queen: *Votorio* collect the votes vpon the hearing of this p^{r}tention;

Votorio goes along & receives all the votes softly & then say aloud.

Voto: All the votes agree for his reception;

Queen: And mine shall confirme all;
Me thinkes both sences are interested in gratitude in his protection: women, for the demonstration of their power: & men for the exaltation of their Loves,

Mor: My admission here, is such a blessing as it charmes all my former wishes, & removes me from the probability of er'e remembring the frustration of them;

1414] page number in lower left corner surrounded by blots 1431 *Sanctuary*] *r* blotted 1435 *depression*] ^{2}*e* altered over indecipherable letter 1439 *say*] for *says* 1442 *sences*] *sexes* BSl

But as

39 [*37)*]

But as a benefitt wch frees me now from wishing any thing; [Fol. 21b]

Queene. Let the oath be given him, & the habitt, & this Convocation dismiss'd;

Hee kisses the Queenes hand
& is saluted by all the ladyes

Exeunt omnes.

Finis Actus secundi.

40.

The Song [Fol. 22a]
after the second Act.

Heere meritorious humblenes doth rise
Vp from a Pallace to a Paradice.
And who would call it lesse, now they have seene.
The heavenly residence of a beauteous Queene.
There is noe Eye that wonder leaves a voyce.
That must not be the Adorer of his Choyce.
For every one, will see that shee alone.
Was beautyes Queene before she had a throne.
Soe beautyes partials't servant must concurr
She hath rais'd Beauty more then Beauty her,
The only wonder this Choyce doth infuse
Is that there could be such a one to chuse.
The proofe of the strange vertue of this place.
To ease misfortune, '[ti]s not a Cōmon case
They that can find out nothing heare to please
Have a misfortune, that deserves noe ease.

41

1447] incorrect page no. *37* just visible under blotted deletion, lower right corner; *39* written to left, blotted   1448 *any*] *a* blotted   Fol. 22a] decorative flourish under end of song   1471 *'[ti]s*] *ti* (though not the dot) scratched out, unnecessary preceding comma retained

Act: 3 · [FOL. 22b]

Scene: 1 ·

Genorio:

42.

Geno: Since the expulsion of that light, that lighted me out – [FOL. 23a] of my selfe, I finde my selfe setling againe into my owne temper, & the dispute is reduc'd now only to my memory: ~//⌒ *ffidamira* doth p^{r}vayle having the deeper seate; my eyes had drawne a superficiall darkenes over, which had but overshadow'd not displac'd my ffidamira: & I finde those shadowes vanish'd – now, being removed out of those beames that made them: ⌒ Therefore now I will first goe & take out the staynes of those new colours, wch my eyes had lett into my heart, & guild my thoughts over anew wth ffidamira's rayes; on wch noe other beames shall ever shine, but to make them glister more; Oh that the Princes stay may setle his passion as much as my departure hath setled mine! soe shall this Iourney doubly ⌒ secure my Fidamira; I will first visitt her, & from thence – dispatch trusty Inquirers into severall parts to discover the aboad of this wilde Princesse of Navarr; & vpon any discovery I will repaire vnto the Prince;

Enter Fidamira disguis'd like a Moore.

Fidam: The kings impatient search hath followed me soe fast, as it hath been my habitt, not my leggs, that hath sav'd me from surprizall; Here comes one, but his easy [<—>] pace implyes he followes noe body;
The Gods guide you S^{r} towards your desire;

Geno: Asmuch good fortune wayte on all your wishes; Lady;

ffidam: It may be S^{r} you may contribute much to mine in the – direction of my way: by a certaine knowledge of wch my hast, would be advantag'd: Knowe you S^{r} the – way to the Shepheards *Paradice*?

1481 *superficiall*] written as *super ficiall* *over,*] *over it* BSl *which*] *wh* heavily inked, altered 1485 *colours*] *r* blotted 1489 *mine!*] head of *!* poorly formed, written over a comma 1498] erasure damage covered by one line, no visible letters

Geno: You are in your direct way Lady? my owne im̄ediate comeing from thence may assure you of it: one daies Iourney will seate you there;

Your.

43

Fidam: Your comeing from thence S^{r} may informe me of ~ – somewhat may more advance me then the p^{r}sent p*ro*secution of my Iourney if yor owne hast p*er*mitt you; [FOL. 23b]

Geno: Though I move not vpon my owne occassions, yet they are soe addrest to the service of your sex, as I dare allow you any time you shall demaund;

Fidam: Sure S^{r} you are much indebted to our sex, that thinke you owe somuch civility to me, that seeme to be one of those that ⌢ – nature hath appointed for a punishment thus to mourne for Beautyes Martyrs;

My curiosity shall not presume too much, since it is seconded wth such a face; I would only knowe whether you were there at the last Election of the Queene: & how the forme is of receiving those into the society, that desire admission;

Geno: I owe the sex somuch Lady, as I am confident I shall not adde one to the number of those you call mourners; But me thinkes your blacke becomes you soe well as if Beauty it selfe (weary of white & redd) had retir'd a while to blacke for a variety; I can resolve you Lady of the Election of the Queene, whoe is called *Bellessa*, & having heard the Lawes read at the Coronation, can instruct you in the forme of receiving p^{r}tenders into the Society, wch is by the ~//~ – manifestation of some case wherein vertue pressed by — ffortune into an extremity brings off her selfe intire, and flyes thither for Sanctuary;

Fidam: I doubt not then of being receiv'd vnles my birth prove – such a misfortune as may make me vnfitt for that ~//~ – beautuous society; wch I heare are all such they need not a foyle to set them off, otherwise my misfortunes are such as it may seeme a shame to vertue to be subiect to soe many;

Geno: Vertue Madam is alwayes in Hostility against many Enemyes; & even her scarrs doe not impaire her, but make her still entirer; Therefore she suffers nothing by her lyablenes to distresse,

1511 *yor*] *o* inked twice, paper damage under ^{r}, where a letter has probably been erased 1536 *beautuous*] for *beauteous* 1537 *otherwise*] written as *other wise* 1541 *Therefore*] written as *There fore*

Fidam: Is the Queene Sr that is, to be chosen most by her beauty: vnquestionably the handsomest of the society? [Fol. 24a]

Geno: She is such a one Lady, as will oblige you somuch, as to make you equall wth the rest of the Society; All of them compar'd to her there is (in my minde) soe much Disparity, as all Companions reach neere alike; she put me that was arm'd wth love (I thought of proofe agt the world) to flight, to save my selfe;

Fidam: You have forgott nothing then Sr that I may serve you in, in recompence of this Civility?

Geno: Yes Lady, I have forgot that there, wch I hope I shall never remember more, but as a danger, from wch, I owe the Gods thankes for my delivery; you will finde there A Shepheard called Moramante, lately received, Hee was a freind of mine, to him you may be pleas'd to prsent the wishes of his freind that left him lately;

Fidam: I thinke Sr our hast may now part vs vpon equall termes, they both seem'd to require the prosecution of our way;

Geno: The gentlenes of your Conversation Lady, & the Harshnes of yor Condition both seeme to neede & deserve this wish which I will leave wth you;

May all your Ioyes have leisure, sorrowes Hast,
your wishes only by successe displac't:

Exeunt

Scen: 2 ·
Pantamora:

Pant: How vnsure are the calmest Harbours mortality can Anchor in? ffortune hath rays'd a storme for me, that drives me even out of this security: & makes the exposure of my selfe to the wyde Ocean of the world againe, A wish for safety; My sincking here, is now inevitable; and this safe discent is more vnsufferable to me then hanging on a rocke, & soe to perish wth the preheminence; The sad misfortune wch ⌒ admitted me into this Sanctuary, is soe outvy'de by this, that's

1546 *All of them*] not in BSl 1547 *Companions*] *Comparisons* BSl 1548 *neere*] ~ *her* FCos; *her* BSt, BPet, 8°
1561 *Condition*] written as *Cond ition* 1572 *inevitable*] written as *in evitable* *discent*] cramped

fallen on me now, as even this place that did releive me then, becomes my p*er*secution;

Here I *45)*

[FOL. 24b]

Here I found ease for all the paines that spightfull Death, by his cursed seizure on my love, inflicted on mee: But here's none, for the extinction of my power; Love is not soe ~ —— irremediable a [<–––>] passion as Ambition is, Love when it growes lesse Annihilates it selfe, & soe becomes it's owne remedy; but ambition yeilds not to repulse, but rises vpp —– againe as often, as it is throwne downe, & soe is lesse ~//⌒ – releiveable: All the Comfort I can admitt of is this, that my vexation doth soe renew a thing, as to defeate the peacefull vertue of this place: though, that wilbe much abated by the necessity of my dissembling of my Discontents, Here comes Melidoro & Camæna, they are soe pleas'd, they will easily be deceiv'd

Enter Melidoro Camæna.

Cam: Wee may give you Pantamora, asmuch Ioy in the resignation of your power, as Bellessa in the possession: since shee can enioy, but what you have done; & she cannot enioy what you doe now (your selfe) till she resigne that;

Pant: I don't repine Camena, at my Resignation; but 'tis to avoyd a sinne, not that I p^{r}ferr a private Condition before soe publick an Eminence: ffor I beleive the possession of ones selfe, is — much enlarg'd by the extent of power; Active thoughts – Camena, are not to be wearyed but by ease; They that preferr retreats & privacyes for the enioying of themselves, cousen themselves of what they might improve in Company: & soe it may be, loose more in that they might acquire, then in that they make vse of in the easynes of their contentednes; Sure for the prospect of my thoughts, I would choose an – Eminence to sett them on;

Melid: Sure Pantamor if our thoughts take their Horizon att a convenient distance, the o͞missi͞on of them soe farr is a recreation to them; But if they looke soe farr as to meete noe termination but the ayre: they loose themselves

1579 *inflicted*] written as *in flicted* 1581] erasure damage covered by blotted horizontal strokes; tail of preceding *a* appears to have been joined to a now invisible letter 1582 *Annihilates*] ^{2}*a* blotted 1585 *All*] *A* oddly formed, perhaps false start 1586 *renew*] *newe* BSl 1587 *though, that*] perhaps initially *thought*; *h* and *t* joined, with comma under the joining stroke, ^{1}*t* of *that* inked twice 1595 *Resignation*] *R* blotted 1599 *preferr*] *pr* blotted, poor nib 1607 *omission*] *emission* FCos, BSt, BPet, 8°

in their extent; Privacy may send out thoughts as farr as a Conspicuous exaltation;

46) Therefore

Therefore sure, they that in a calme solitude can keepe their wishes wthin their reach, & their thoughts wthin their wishes: enioy as much happines as they can thinke of, & none desire more; [FOL. 25a]

Cam: But it seemes Pantamora, 'tis not the Peace but the priority you affect among vs; & that this place had only the vertue [to] of ease to you, as it was capable of Soveraignty, not devoted – vnto solitude;

Pant: Mistake me not Camæna, I doe not thinke it cheapens private Ioyes, to rayse the value thus of her's, that even the Gods ⌜in⌝tend advantage to; But I forgive you that by the estimation of – your owne happines, cannot consent to allow soveraigntye ⌢ precedency; you will better vnderstand one another, therefore I'le leave you; *Exit*.

Melid: Give me leave Camena, wth an humble patience to demaund why you would not consent to a Dismission this late Election;

Cam: The deferring of your remove from hence, contynues you – Melidoro in your throne, for possession (they say) much more propriety entrenches on loves prerogative; The Impropriation of our selves proves vs more habitable but lesse delightfull, & the fervency of your love would thereby coole to a teppid warmth, wch is not only voyd of brightnes but of light: Love is darkened Melidoro, when the flame is put out;

Melid: Hymens torches doe imply, Camena, Loves Lampe is nourisht not put out, & may not love blaze aswell in them as Cupids wilde desires;

Cam: They say indeed they are the Emblems of the nuptiall flames, wch goe out i'th morning;

Melid: All flames Camena, as they be lightsome, soe to me are wavering too; wee see their light and their vncertaine motion both at once; Therefore suppose this flame of love put out by nuptiall rites; It setles them into a temporate heate, whose equall ardor purifyes it more: for love like

1612 *Therefore*] distantly joined, perhaps intended as *There fore* 1621 *⌜in⌝tend*] *in* interlined with caret 1622 *I forgive*] *I f* blotted by damage to paper on verso 1623] slanting vertical line at end of line, perhaps deleting punctuation 1626 *patience*] *pa* heavily inked 1641 *lightsome*] *so* blotted

Gold, Camena, must be brought to a fluidnes, & so by receiving an Impression; becomes most vsefull;

In 47)

Cam: In this vsefullnes you speake of, the Gold is made lighter still, & is made currant by Allay: soe women like Gold loose of their [<)()()(>] value, for the good they doe: I cannot yet resolve to abate somuch from what I love soe well my selfe: as a submission to propriety; [Fol. 25b]

Melid: Nuptiall bonds Camena, doe not convey you over to the propriety of him they are delivered to, they rather doe inlarge the ⌢ – owning of selfe: for they make that wch you vouchsafe to ioyne vnto it, the same as your selfe; Doe not fright me then Camena wth that word [C<...)()(>] submission, when all I wish by this Identity is, to become more subiect to you: for wee dispose nothing our selves.

Enter Votorio:

Voto: Melidoro & Camena I come to warne you both to the ⌢ – Convocation: The Queene hath appointed this day for the hearing of a new pretender; the hower is neare att hand;

Mel: Cam: Wee will both goe along;

Exeunt.

Scen: 3 ·
Enters Fidamira now called Gemella:

Gemel: Now am I secur'd from those feares of the kings pursuite (least I should once enioy a thoughtlesse ease) I finde a new care rise vp before me: How I should disguise my story? ffortune hath provided such an excesse for me as I must spare the halfe, least my distresse should seeme soe immedicable as to exclude me from this ease; The strangenes of my curse is such, as my complaint may

1650] erasure damage causing holes, three blotted flourishes covering 1657] head of *C* just visible; otherwise the erasure has caused such severe damage that the quantity of missing letters cannot be seen, though the deleted word was probably *Camena*, repeated from four words before; there has also been an attempt to cover the damage with flourishes *submission*] lower loop of *s* blotted by preceding damage 1659 *nothing*] *nothing so freely as* BSl

seeme a vanity; not a deiection; to alledge the love of Princes for a misfortune? Therefore I must degrade them of that quality, & relate them but as ffather & sonne;

Enter Queene & Society)

The

48·

Queen: The Pretender is already here. let's take our places and give her audience; [Fol. 26a]

Gemel: The very introduction to my story, Ladyes, may be p^{r}tence enough vnto your pitty; in that I am reduc'd to begg beleife of you in that, wch above all derogates from yor selves: That your contrariety could be beloved; And that which will avert you Gentlemen from the credit of it, is, that it may seeme a scandall to have this love imputed on men, vnto whose colours this of mine must seeme a staine, & not an Ornam^{t} Thus am I soe miserable as before I plead my Cause to make my Iudges iustly parties ag^{t} me; But this wonder past & pardon'd, the Consequents may be the easyer beleev'd, although successively vnnaturall a ffather, & a sonne being the subiects of this wonder; The passion of the sonne was first, the fathers followed it, vnseene vnto the sonne; The father made the first discovery & in a rage resolv'd to cutt of his sonnes life; This was all the mercy that the Iury Iealousy would allow the son, The ffather (as it seemes) being p*er*swaded by it, that – the blacknes of these his thoughts, would fitly match the colour wherewth nature hath suited me; The fathers horrid purpose was soe resolute, that finding me one day constantly vnmoov'd, wthall those stormes, Lovers Complaints doe rayse: at last his swelling sadnes broake into a rage that would revenge; He said, since nature had curs'd him vnto the makeing of his curse, his sonne, by whose makeing his owne end was destin'd; – – ⌒ Therefore his thoughts condemn'd his sonne of more then parricide, His intercepting of my love to him; And he should be sacrific'd to this suspicion, soe litle did hee love, twice him selfe set by his love to mee, —

1689 *on*] *vnto* BSl 1697 *vnseene*] written as *vn seene* 1699 *Iury*] *fury* FCos, BSt, BPet, 8°

And this he said he did acquaint me wth, that my

vertue

49·

vertue (wch had byn his Tormentor) might have the – [Fol. 26b] paine of being the Cause, & knowing this detestable – effect wthout the meanes of prevention, wch his instant execution should make impossible: & thus he seem'd to fly from me, as if the pleasure of this act already, had —– displac't[<.>] that of loving me, & being wth me; Then I (councell'd by vertue wch had noe power to divert this rage) disguis'd her into a shape wch might please this fury for a while, & soe delude it by its owne resemblance, I ⌢ ⌢ pursuing him wth a fury like his, stayed him, seemeing to follow & imbrace his rage, not wrastle wth it; I told him thus; I did allow this brave resolve of his, high ⌢ – enough to iustefy my yeilding to, And I could ne're have thought to have met a humour worthy the matching mine vnto; I told him mine was none of those tender hearts, – that sighes could blow into a flame, it had an Adamantive temper, wch only blood could soften, And that he had done like the painter, that had made the picture of a Lyon running mad, & wanting nothing but the foame to – – represent, grew soe distracted wth dispaire of hitting of it as in a rage he threw his pencill at it, & by this chance did rarely perfect his abandon'd worke; And soe his fury had (throwing it selfe into soe high dispaire) made vp that figure wch only could take me; Therefore he that could intend to kill his sonne, to impossibilitate his Ioyes, will easily doe it to assure them: wch if he will promise: on the beleife of his brave minde, he should have possession of me this night, before the Ceremoniall rights; He agreed to this wth somuch Ioy, he seem'd to thinke he had made not destroy'd a sonne; Then I sent instantly vnto the sonne & (by tokens that I had taken from the father as pledges of his word) ⌢ assur'd him his death was purpos'd by his ffather & that

1719 *displac't[<.>]* cross-stroke of *t* missing owing to erasure which has caused a small hole; thick horizontal stroke covers gap before *that* 1726 *And*] *A* heavily inked, with cross-stroke, over an indecipherable letter *have*] false start, perhaps on *l* 1735 *perfect*] *p* poorly formed where nib has split on the descender

50. night;

night; And that there did remaine noe time for him to doe any thing but fly, this he beleiving did flye – - instantly; wch I assur'd of, my next part was now to vn=maske my vertue whose vizard was offensive; Therefore wing'd wth Innocence I did resolve to flye, over those Seas wch p*ar*t our neighborring Islands: leaving a letter wch ⌒ might cleare my vertue, from that black Ingagemt: I had made: & coming hither the kind Gods presented me, wth the report of this Divine aboad, wch offers it selfe equally to the releife of all the distrest of all Nations & sexes; Thus have you heard a story whose strangenes needs somuch your pitty, it must first aske yor Creditt, as a Charity: wch if you vouchsafe, I cannot doubt a faire Comiseration; [FOL. 27a]

Queen: *Votorio* Collect the votes.

He Collects them & sayes

Voto: No vote opposeth the Admission, but one.

Queen Whose?

Moram: 'Tis myne Madam, that doth dissent only for a fitter pitty to this vnhappy Lady, for she seemes arm'd wth a minde brave enough not to esteeme this residence an ease, that shall exclude her from the Dignity of the Queene: wch her p*er*son wee know doth debarr her heere being a Moore; if she can lett her selfe fall into these priudices, shee shall have my vote, to me more pittyed after her admission then before;

Queen: You have fayl'd Moromante in both parts.

Can nature be accus'd of spight
for having made both day & night?
That wch is iniur'd by Comparison,
Must be Comparable or can have none,

The.

51

The Contrarietyes of nature, are [FOL. 27b]
made for their apposition, not compare;
The Darkenes of the night may be as faire.
for it, as can the dayes serenest ayre

1770 *admission*] *sion* cramped   1778 *apposition*] *opposition* BSl

And soe this coulour of it selfe may bee
Lovely as our's in it's owne Degree;

And for the exclusion of her selfe from hope of being Queene, she doth noe more then all of vs, submitt to the opinion of the most, & whoe knowes what one day may be called beauty? since wee see the opinion of it alter every day; *Votorio* let the Lawes be read to her, & the oath administred;

Gemel: Nature Madam hath by my humility, enlightned soe the darke misfortune of my birth, as Ambition my Contrariety, seemes soe lovely vnto me, as I shall wish nothing but rest and solitude, whose shades best fitt me;

Exeunt

Scen: 4·
King.

King Oh *ffidamira*, thy feares have blemisht even thy – Innocence, in this iniust afflixion of thy Prince, that had noe thought, but how to shew that Princes are happy in the meanes of setting vertue in it's truest Lustre; if needlesse – feares did shake thee into this remove out of thy ffathers howse, 'twas thy humility, that did not knowe that thy – transcendent meritt was somuch, that a King could not spare the smallest Circumstance in all his power, to - honour it enough: for what I was forc't to doe to avoid omission: thou didst avoyd for an excesse, was it not paine enough for me to part wth Basilino, wthout the addition of this strange curse?

That

52.

That his retorne should prove a Torment to me? for soe it must in this distresse of ffidamira; Oh that hee were come back! that I might free the name of King from such misfortune, & resigning to his guiltlesse youth, breake off this thred of life by ruder motion, & not stay till it wore [FOL. 28a]

1789 *my Contrariety*] *whose* ~ BSl, FCos; *whose couler is* ~ BSt; *whose collour is my contrary* BPet, 8° 1790 *lovely*] *vnlovely* FCos, BSt, BPet, 8° 1796 *iniust*] for *vniust* 1799 *ffathers*] cramped, with no space between [1]*f* and preceding *y* 1806 *curse*] *r* blotted, not well formed

out wth age; most of them I sent in seach of him, already - are returned, & wth their silent sadnes, bring mourning only for their answere;
Into how wilde a Deviation have my straying sorrowes lead me? they have brought me here alone vnto away, - whose shady mellancholly seemes to invite me to beginn my Pilgrimage; Heere comes on too whose lookes forespeake his newes; what have you found her?

Genorio sadly disguis'd

Geno: Who should I have found?

King: Cans't thou looke soe, & aske me who? is there soe much sorrow left in all the rest o'th world, as thou pretend'st too, & not imployed on ffidamira? what art thou that – – seems't soe boldly sad, to vey wth me?

Geno: This is the king I must dissemble;
I am one that may allow you any subiect you can choose vnto your selfe, & then dispute afflixion wth you; I am a voted Pilgrim whose wandring motions seeke theire ayme, hopeles of somuch rest, as even the knowledge of the end they are directed too;

King Alas thou art soe short of me, as even thy misery is my wish; were it in my Choyce to be a Pilgrim, or a King, I would choose thy curse, for ease: if you have nothing els to vye wth me, you may add this vnto your greifes (if [they] you did meane they should exceede all others) the being out sorrowed now by me;

My:

53

[FOL. 28b]

Geno: My sorrowes S^{r} doe lye soe heavy on me, I cannot rayse them vp soe high as a relation: yours must be lighter needes since you can lift them vp soe high as to yor mouth;

King This dumbe silence vnder the pressure of afflixion may — aswell imply your weakenes as your sorrowes weight, Therefore rayse your Complaints soe high to put them in a ballance ag^{t} mine to try wch out weigh;

Geno: I am content (to lighten yours) to weigh wth you: I have

1812 *seach*] for *search* *him*] *her* BPet, 8° 1816 *away*] for *a way* 1818 *forespeake*] *ake* in margin, *ke* cramped 1828 *choose*] *oose* cramped

lov'd: & have been soe neare enioying, as the disappointm^{t} did double the paine; by the reflex of that wch light on her, I lov'd by this deferring of our Ioyes, wch I am now more distanc'd from, then I was ever neere;

King: I did resist & overcame a passion, whose opposition had left but one paine in all the world greater then it, and that fell on me; The disappointment of my love for whose successe I only could have yeilded: & I remaine guilty in the opinions of them both, as the defeater of their Ioyes; The one I shall never see againe to vndeceive, the other I must see soe guiltily deceived as he vniustly must condemne his ffather;

Geno: This is the only misery I doe confesse, that I could allow a pitty to, I doe allow you S^{r} full advantage as I doe confesse your present misery is above my feare, But give me leave (a stranger to your Countrey & to yor story) to aske whether that ffidamira that you nam'd at first be yet alive? me thinkes her death might ease you much;

King: Kind Pilgrim in the absence of my son, my cursed care & fate guided her the only way vnto my guilt, her flight; I doe not thinke her dead, more then a Disguise may be a p^{r}paration to it; soe as death may have a better — p^{r}tence to seize her then, as not her herselfe, then in the lively illustration of herselfe, And to let the see, Kind Pilgrim how due to this thy ingenious yeilding was, I will direct thee;

54 *To an*

[FOL. 29a]

To an ease of all thy miseryes, while mine owne are vnreleivable; you have heard sure of the *Shepheards Paradice*, whose peacefull bounds have that strange vertue from the Gods, as to include all those that are admitted there, in peacefull acquiescence, Thither repaire: for though you have not greife enough to weigh wth mine: yet are your misfortunes full enough, to be receiv'd; And when you finde the smiles of that smooth place, laugh at yor wrinckled sorrowes past, then for my sake, dispute your

1847 *disappointm^{t}*] m^{t} in margin 1848 *light*] *litt* FCos only 1864 *alive?*] *?* altered from semi-colon, comma remaining as point *thinkes*] written as *thin kes* 1871–2 *And . . . thee*] cramped horizontally and vertically 1877 *acquiescence*] *ui* has only two minims, but is dotted

Ioyes wth those contented soules;

Geno: I will submitt my steps to your direction S^{r} but to an end differing soe farr from what you doe prescribe, as mine shalbe in a Defyance vnto Peace; I will even there rayse vp new sorrowes, wch my distracted soule shall there erect for Trophees got from the contesting vertue of that place;

King: ffollow my Councell freind, It may be the vertue of that place may be soe strange it will not aske somuch as yor owne willingnes towards your releife. I must leave you:

Exit.

Geno: The Gods be wth you Sr And may you live to be a wonder in the contrary extreame of what you are; Alas good King how patient have I been to allow your sorrowes, — victory, striving wth mine, wch those were that you – – brought forth, for ffidamira's flight belongs to me, & hath noe Comfort but the Admiration of her vertue, wch this happy meeting of the King hath soe ~ ~ exalted, as the wonder mingles wth the sence of my disappointment, & soe tempers it into a hopefull – patience; I will goe back directly to the Prince, & nowe assure him the Princesse of Navarr is dead to stopp his farth^{r} search; & as I finde his thoughts fixed or moved from ffidamira, soe contrive his retorne, the wch will quickly reveale my ffidamira, whoe must needs be hid in some neighbo^{r}ing privacy secur'd by her vertuous feare;

This.

55·

[FOL. 29b]

This pennance of not seeing her, I take as due to these faulty Eyes, that have byn pleas'd wth another Obiect, – wch now redeem'd, shall make me watch their straying motions wth a stricter care;

Beauty shall slide of from them as it falls;
Lyke smooth things lighting vpon Christall balls.
Whos touch does part, & not togethe fixe.

1885 *there*] cramped 1886 *there*] cramped 1891 *leave*] head of *a* carelessly formed 1898 *noe*] *e* not well formed 1901 *hopefull*] *hope* and *full* distantly joined, *full* perhaps added after completion of word 1904 *farth^{r} search*] without space, ^{r} almost above *s* 1915 *Whos*] for *Whose* *togethe*] for *together*

Their owne agreeing makes they cannot mixe:
Soe Beauty in my Eyes shall meete wth such:
It cannot fixe but passe as it doth touch:
Exit:

Scene: 5.
Bellessa: Moromante: [Melidoro]: Martiro

Queene: That wch you reported of the Prince Moromante is now confirm'd by this Lady that wee admitted; she past that way, she said & describes his passion, & his parts, it seemes a miracle that faith or honour could have vertue enough to resist his will;

Moro: I knowe the Prince Madam well: & I beleive where ever hee is gone, heaven will direct him to a Choyce;

Betweene wch & his owne, there shalbe asmuch odds
As is betwixt his choosing, & the Gods:

Queen: You beleive then Moromante he will love againe, you ⌒– thinke (it seemes) heaven doth allow of loving twice;

Moro: Our mindes are but loves pupills at the first Madam, wch fitt themselves but to proceed & take degrees: soe not by the first stepp but by a gradation, love ascends vnto it's height;

[*Melido:*] *Martiro* I will allow you Moromante love is noe Irradiation of a light into our soules, whose first instant brightnes in it's perfection: but may not the first sparkes be kept alive and raysed vnto as high a light as can the second? wch is kindled still by putting out the first;

'Tis

56

Mor: 'Tis not an extinction of the flame, Martiro, 'tis but a — [FOL. 30a] Change of the materiall, that fomented it, soe second loves have this advantage, the being the first instant in that — height, the first was long a growing too; wch must prove it higher, The having gott above it;

Queene: These Degrees of Elevation, Moromante, you require in

1938 *in it's*] *is* ~ BSl

love, inferr this consequence that love should be a contynued motion, by change aspireing to trancendency; Therefore he is to blame that takes but one, for, by your inference, the number must exalt the last vnto the greatest height, your inconstancy doth not concerne vs soe, as you should strive to prove it a vertue to vs;

Morom: In this Degree Madam wch I have nam'd love comes to touch a point after wch all motion is declination: I doe not allow loves lightnes, or variety contributes to its height Had I thought inconstancy a vertue Madam, I ne're had byn bless'd wth this soe great a Ioy as seeing you;

Queene: I doe confesse the Prince, for many reasons, might not be allowed but wish'd a second & delightfull choyce, that hee may knowe our sex hath Ioyes, that may outprize his – - sufferrings: hee may els grow vaine in this his sorrow & beleeve love owes him more, then it can pay in all our sex;

Mor: What say you then to my Condition, whose sufferings I should thinke iniur'd compar'd wth his; might not I — p^{r}tend to have my second choyce, call'd wisdome, not inconstancy?

Queen: I beleive you might & I should pitty you the more, were you not here in this delightfull ease;

Mor: You speake Madam as though you wish'd him here, where would he were, even in my place, & I any where, but wth your pitty;

You

57
[FOL. 30b]

Queene: You wish Moromante much against him, and more - against your selfe, for you had my pitty in your admittance, at first sight;

Mor: If I wish him Madam in my place, 'tis that I dare — wish more in his name, then in my owne: in whom soe insolent a wish as your esteeme, could finde but such a pitty as distraction doth;

Queene: I doe esteeme you so much Moromante, as I dare resolve never to pitty you; somuch I trust the vertuous peace of our compos'd & setled thoughts;

1948 *inferr*] written as *in ferr* 1961 *outprize*] distantly joined 1969 *were*] cramped 1971 *would*] cramped 1982 *our*] *your* BSl *compos'd*] loop of ascender of *d* blotted

Mart: *Moromante*, is soe civill Madam, he would make the vertue of this place defective, to endeare your power; by the applying of his wishes vnto you; & your civility to vs Madam, is such you borrow now this time from your devotions;

Queen: 'Tis true Martiro tymes not soe civill as to stay for any body; *Exit*

Mor: I have not yet devotion enough Madam to forgive Martiro his excesse, i'le stay behinde a litle to dispose my selfe [of] to that; I see there is noe vizarding of love, to make it – passe abroad vnknowne, the eye or mouth are even – – enough to shew what 'tis, Nay did young love it selfe wish a disguise, it could not ever be fitted; for, whoe can take measure of a growing love? where every instant adds asmuch as even our thoughts can comprehend; & now love seemes to promise me advantage by this selfe discovery, it prompts me to Martiro's freindshipp, whose trust will both afford my love more roome for recreacon of it selfe, & helpe to carry it neerer Bellessa, by an – - insensible reproach wch it may make him; I will

58 professe

professe my passion freely to Martiro, I'me sure to be beleiv'd that's a Ioy, wch I defye my owne misfortune to oppose me in; [FOL. 31a]

All love's a light, wch as it doth eiect
Shadowes, by them it doth it selfe detect:
Soe he that thinkes love can be shadow'd quite
Knowes not there is noe shadow wthout light;

He lets fall a paper. *Exit.*

Scen: 6 ·
Gemella:

Gem: Is this strange discovery part of my curse? my findeing

1990 *Martiro*] cramped 1993 *abroad*] written as *a broad* 1999 *freindshipp*] ^{2}*i* gone over twice to delete indecipherable letter beneath; ^{1}*p* blotted 2000 *recreacon*] cramped 2002 *reproach*] *approach* BSl 2004 *misfortune*] *une* cramped

out of the Prince, only, that I might misse Agenor? The peace this place affords had been too much for me; wthout this disquiet of Agenors p*ar*ting wth the Prince; I can – guesse noe reason vnles he should (finding him setled here) have ask'd leave to goe back vnto the king, wth the designe of seeing me; wch I am aptest to suspect it does soe well agree wth my misfortunes; yet some divining thoughts promise me, I shall here redeeme the Princes favour by some strange service: I doe – perceive his passion, & will apply my selfe studiously to pursue his ends; Here lyes a paper, This is the hand: I can't mistake my Eyes are not disguis'd, These are verses full of passion, I will keepe them soe, as she, he meant them to, shall see them more recomended then thus chance could doe; *Exit.*

Scen: 7 ·
Pantamora:

Pant: I thanke my thoughts for this reproach they send me: my love hath once againe master'd by Ambition, & all the Quarrell I have now vnto Bellessa is Moromante's love. I am confident she is already setled there wth all tha'dvantages love can choose, & sure she cannot choose, but see her selfe there by the reflex of his addresses;

wch are 59.

[FOL. 31b]

wch are soe cleere as her connive implyes, she findes her selfe noe way disfigur'd there; now my thoughts — shall take their rise noe lower then the Admiration of her Beauty, & her vertues, & from thence, carry my loves successe above them all; I will not strike on flat of envy or detraction; but in faire conspicuous sleights will — worke above her; *Exit.*

Moromante.

Mor: To what a rashnes hath my love transported me? as if I might expect my passion had given me an equall power

2024 *the*] *his* FCos, BSt, BPet, 8° 2025 *disguis'd,*] unusually long comma; perhaps a semi-colon from which the pen has not been lifted 2032 *by*] *my* BSl 2033–5 *I . . . addresses*] lines cramped horizontally and vertically 2034 *tha'dvantages*] written as one word 2041 *sleights*] *flightes* BSt, BPet, 8°

[<—>] over others, to that it has assum'd over me, I did – deliver vp my wishes to Martiro, wth such a Confidence as if I had granted his Contribution to them as a suit: & he answered me wth such a cold civility as did imply surprize; He said he wondred that soe noble a passion, could be [<~~>] defective in soe essentiall a point as secrecy; but that he would impute this opening of my selfe to him to a desire of makeing him a freind, in this confidence ⌜in⌝ [<–>] him, by the exposure of my hapynes to his discretion, In fine hee – promis'd me my love should be lock'd wth the p*ro*foundest secretts of his hidden thoughts, wch should ne're have more ayre then [<~~~>] ⌜would⌝ afford them breath to live, but not to speake; how dull was I not to beleive before, that all were in love wth her? All women must needs envy her, & all men me for out loving them;

Enter Genorio led by twoe Souldiers.

Sould: Wee may discharge our selves of this charge having mett wth you S^{r} whoe are of the society;

Mor: This stranger freinds is addrest to me, where you may leave him: take your discharge;

Sould: Wee obey S^{r} & leave you:

60 *Dost thou*

Mor: Dost thou bring newes Genorio, that thou hadst rather thy [FOL. 32a] Cloathes should tell then thou? what blacke traverse hast – thou brought betweene me & my Ioyes, wch were ready to embrace thee?

Geno: I am vnhappy S^{r} to come to be embrac'd by you in this infectious colour, wch must sully & blacke you too;

Mor: Throw then Genorio quickly those blackes over me, for nothing can appeare soe vgly vnto me, as doth this party colour'd doubt;

Geno: If the black be not soe pollisht, as you may see yo^{r}selfe in it, then let your thoughts sincke downe as lowe as possible

2046] erasure damage covered by single horizontal stroke, no letter visible 2050] erasure damage covered by two flourishes, no letters visible 2053 ^{2}*in*] interlined with caret above deletion, erasure damage covered by single horizontal stroke, no letter visible 2057] erasure damage covered by three flourishes, no letters visible *would*] interlined with caret, mainly above following *afford* 2058–60 *was . . .* ^{1}*her . . . out loving*] the water used for the erasure in 2057 dripped down the page, leaving the paper crinkled, and the ink smudged on *wa*, *er*, and *t lo* 2073 *infectious*] written as *in fectious* 2078 *possible*] *possibly* BSl

you can, & you must needs find your misfortune there; you have not many to confound your Choyce;

Mor: It must be that Genorio wch sinckes beyond the Centure of misfortune, soe as it ascends vpward towards heaven, in a rebellion for Saphira's elevation thither: my distraction tells me it must be that, & iustefyes this seizure on me; I am soe mad already, I doe not wish it should be lesse: & I am not soe happy, as to be naturally mad, I have soe much sence left yet; Genorio, I thanke the for exempting thy selfe from soe foule a cryme as telling me;

Geno: Give me leave to tell you Sr you have not guest soe much misfortune, as your distraction goes now about to make; — suppose heavenly Saphira at her home; will not the part of Lamentation you owe her, aske an entire soule to pay it? why doe you then teare that in peeces, wch even whole will be too litle? doe you thinke that lesse then a man can be enough to mourne for?

Mor: As I am my selfe Genorio, I must needs be the vnfitter to mourne for her; for soe I owe her most; should I seeke to save those sences, wch are guilty of her death? no Genorio, noe lesse then running mad, & byteing even the vertue of this place, soe as by my infliction, it may distracted dye; & turne this Paradice into a mourning wildernes, where

nothing

61)

nothing but wilde sorrow should abide: There's nothing but the inversion of this place, & the vertue of it, can bee a monument of greife enough for the Divine Saphira; [FOL.32b]

offers to goe away

But stay Genorio, before I goe, tell me the manner of her leaving of this world: That I may be higher swolne wth this blacke rageing poyson, I must spread: That it may or'ecome all those Antidotes, this place is strengthned with;

Geno: The knowledge of this Circumstance wilbe soe vsefull to you

2094] increasing problems with a poor nib throughout this speech have left several letters in this line blotted: *do* of *doe*, *h* of *thinke*, *th* of *that*, *th* of *then* 2095 *mourne for*] ~ *her* BSl 2096 *selfe*] *f* heavily inked, perhaps altered 2100 *infliction*] written as *in fliction*

Sr as you must give me leave now to Condition for the imparting it: since you are not your selfe I neede not – owne my Duty: Therefore promise Sr to reassume soe much sence as to comply wth your owne duty, & your – deare ffathers wishes: whose sorrow for your absence — ioyning wth his age, will quickly rob you of some of those your dedicated greifes: & require A great share for him; Therefore your Duty to Saphira, should advise you to avoyd soe sad a mixture, as his death must be, wch must part greifes wth her;

Mor: Doth my ffather summon me Genorio, to the performance of my word, in my returne? I will begin at this great height of straying nature, my Disobedience to him; I ⌒ must benight the Lustre of this place: Courts of ~// ⌒ themselves are sad enough Genorio, each one hath there his owne p*ar*ticuler afflixion that benummes him; Noe – Genorio it must be here among these Ioyes, where greife's a miracle, I will give black to all this Society; if you will leave me to guesse the manner of her death, I'le shew I am soe starke mad, that I'le beleeve shee dyed for love;

Geno: I'le contribute Sr somuch to the madnes of this beleife, as to lett you knowe she dyed marryed to the king of Albion, whome her beauty (wch was only vndisguiz'd in her -

62 retreate

retreate into his Countrey, wch she chose for solitude) [FOL. 33a] tooke, & rays'd her to the Publicke Eminence of Queene, wthout the helpe of any other quality; All wch vntill her death, they kept conceal'd;

Mor: This may allay my greife into a sober mellancholly: wch I must now impose vpon my selfe; the only meanes of ⌒ – expiation left; This (me thinckes) hath brought me to my selfe againe; Her having been anothers; & now Genorio I will promise the to stay, to vse the vertue of this place, for the recovery of this sad disease; Therefore pretend thou to be admitted here, & I will promise wthin few moneths to declare my selfe, & soe returne, I'le goe & send Votorio to you; *Exit.*

2122 *performance*] *ance* cramped   2131 *love*] *love of mee* FCos, BSt, BPet, 8°   2145 *few*] *a few*] BSl

Geno: I will obey you S^{r}
Sure this p^{r}tence of staying here to mourne, was but –
found out as the best disguise love can put on; I will ⌢
apply my observation & Curiosity to discover, whether
his thoughts are not more fixed on Bellessa's life, then
on Saphira's death;

Votorio:

Voto: The Gods protect you Sr *Moromante* told me you ~// ⌢
demaunded me;
Geno: Hee hath obliged me S^{r} in soe speedy approveing this
favour;
I am come to intreate your helpe in an Audience, for
the delivery of my p^{r}tence to be admitted into the ⌢
Society; ffortune (since I went from hence) hath soe
intended my persecution, as if my having beene but
here had been a Declaration of my selfe against her;
Therefore now I am come back hither for Sanctuary;
Voto: I shall procure S^{r} a speedy Audience, & wish it favo^{r}able;

Exit.

Is it.

63

Gemella: [FOL. 33b]

Gemel: Is it you S^{r} that have brought this darkenes wth you? that
has or'ecast our brother *Moromante*?
Geno: I answered his Inquiry in somewhat, he desired to – –
knowe abroad; wch if it have afflicted him 'twill add
somewhat to my p^{r}tence: The misfortune of having
byn soe cursed, as to bring sorrow hither; It will bee
in your power Madam, now to repay that, wch you
soe lately were pleas'd to call Civility, my direction
of you hither;
Gemel: That wch helpes you S^{r} to retaine me in yor memory,
may excuse me for you are almost fall[<–>] out of – –
[<~~~>] myne: This blacke made me notorious to you:
& hath disguis'd you to me; It seemes you are owner, or

2164] *Therefore*] written as *There fore* 2178 *fall[<–>]*] no longer visible letters erased at end of *fall* (for *fallen*), paper damage covered by single thick horizontal stroke joined to tail of ^{2}l 2179] considerable erasure damage covered by three blotted flourishes

a great sharer, of part of *Moromante*'s greifes;

Geno: Amongst all my misfortunes I have not this of -- nature: Madam, the being insensible of what freind= shipp should affect me wth; But I wonder it falls soe heavy on him, as to cause this deiection since it is on him, but from another whome it fell on first; 'Tis the Death Madam of the Princesse of Navarr, whome the Prince his master was soe in love wth, as he left even his ffathers Court to aske nothing but her pardon; The story is too long to satisfy you of the Princes reasons;

Votorio:

Voto: The Queene is goeing to the audience seate, & it is time s^{r} for you to move that way;

Exit:

Geno: I follow S^{r} in hope of time enough hereafter to aske your pardon, Lady; *Exit:*

I shall

64

Gemel: I shall meete you presently S^{r} [FOL. 34a]

The Gods should enlarge my soule too, to furnish me with more admiration for the vertue of this place; That I - should live to misse Agenor, to endeare the finding of him here; This is hee, my ioyes tell it better then my eyes; The Prince is heere too, And (least the sence of the Princes Saphira's death should attenuate these Ioyes) the Princes being in love wth the divine Bellessa, is fallen out to make her death as 'twere, a sacrifice to all our lives; This frees the Prince from any scruple of his love, & soe p^{r}pares the wish't successe vnto - Agenor & my selfe; I will conceale my selfe still to Agenor; it is not Iealousy but to doe him right, by this allowance of somuch meritt, as his Constancy must be in this place; And I love him soe, I'de have him out meritt me in what I ⌜only⌝ can alleadge, Constancy; I don't dispaire of Bellessa's taking too; my approaches have been successefull yet;

2186 *from*] *fr* blotted 2212 *only*] interlined with caret

Love's well advanc'd, intrench'd wthin our Eares:
It workes securely seperate from all feares:
If it e're come to parley vnder grownd,
But wth our thoughts, wee likely doe Compound;
Exit.

Scene: 8 ·
Queene: Votorio:
And all the Society:

Moromante.

65

Voto: Moromante by me beggs your Maiestyes pardon for his absence, wch his indisposition hath occasion'd./ [FOL. 34b]

Queen: I am sorry for the iustnes of his excuse, Let the ~⌒ Pretender begin;

Geno: I behold deathes Herald, sent to proclaime a victory wch he hath lately had or'e love, by wch both sexes are defeated; soe as men may feare the being lov'd, and women may iustly leave off loving, since nothing but dying can shew they love enough; I am that wretched hee that shame vnto my sex that was belov'd by such

A she, as had not sinne enough to dye.
But death was faine her vertue to imply:

This Treachery did death vse me wth, whils't I was (as I may say) even in his Company as much as – – Darkenes, & absence represent him; In this separation the deadly sinne of lust, arm'd wth the power of a Prince, did assault the vertue of this matchlesse shee, to save whose life, she gave her owne to death delivering it wth her owne hands, wch being not strong enough to defend her Innocence; After this doe not beleive yt I pretend Admission here for Comfort, but bound to – seeke through all the world, the place wch is the – truest Enemy to lust & death; wch, all consent, is

2227 *I behold*] *Behold* FCos, BSt, BPet, 8° 2239 *matchlesse*] written as *match lesse* 2242 *Innocence*] BSl continues *were stronge enough in the defeate of her owne life, when it stood against her innocence*

this; for that vertue wch foyles the first, defeates the power of the last, Therefore I must implore your ayd in this Case, that in revenge of this Iniurious life, I may live here where every life, is such as despiseth death;

Queene. *Votorio*, Collect the votes.

Voto: They all agree for his Admission;

66 Then

Queen: Then I confirme it too; [Fol. 35a]

But me thinkes death hath not beene soe iniurious as your sence would make it, in this Case: for it seemes to have come in vpon the rescue, not the arrest; & soe wee are interested in your life, as a Record of the vertue of our sex;

Geno: Did I not iustly preferr the estimation of this Place, before the rest of the world, I should have beene a moving Monument, that should have dispers'd her⌢ Epitaph as farr as life would have serv'd to carry me; But since in this one Center, meete all the extended lynes of vertue, that are in this worlds Circumference: Here I have chosen to fixe my selfe, that in a firme consistency, the dimension of this vertue might be trulyer taken here;

Queen: Let him be sworne

Voto: You shalbe obeyed Madam;

Exeunt omnes.

ffinis Actus 3. ij

67

[Fol. 35b]

68

2251 *Votorio, Collect*] *rio* altered, *i* probably inserted, joined to *o* by stroke at top of both letters, 3*o* with unusual final stroke perhaps originally joined to an indecipherable letter beneath *C* which is heavily inked with an intrusive cross-stroke
2259 *Place*] *P* not well formed, descender heavily inked

The song after the third
Act. [Fol. 36a]

Here frighted Innocence for succour flyes:
But is too bold in an averse disguise.
To Beauty; wch she seemes to take soe ill:
She sets herselfe to crosse her dearest will
And soe wth all the power she can make.
Attempts from Innocence her right to take.
And doth succeed; & yet the bless'd event
Is such: as it keepes Beauty Innocent;
Here is much weight & heavynes put on,
'Tis that there severall ioyes may match anon;
And soe each one at the appointed day,
Will be the lighter when they throw't away.
Love seemes as yet declar'd all of one side,
But by degrees he will himselfe Divide:
And equally at last both parts will take:
And soe loose nothing, yet all gainers make;

69

The fourth Act: [Fol. 36b]
Scen: 1·

Moramante alone
wth a paper in his hand,

presently after enters
Gemella:
Queene.

70

Mor: My whole life Saphira should have byn thy Epitaph, had not thy end prvented my beginning; This is an oblation, wch my fancy brings vnto thy memory, wch I will offer to [h] it now; [Fol. 38a]

2285 *they*] *e* heavily inked, perhaps altered Fols. 36b–38a] Fol. 37 is completely blank 2300 *[h]*] loop of ascender clearly visible, remainder of letter deleted with short horizontal strokes; probably *h*, perhaps *k*

Enters Gemella.

Gemel: The Queene Moromante hearing of your indisposition comes to visitt you;

Mor: The Queene Gemella? let her not be soe cruell as soe soone to interrupt my sences, in a sorrow they are paying: The seeing her will set me soe behinde, by such an inter= =poseing ioy, as will soe lighten all I can pay after it, that nothing will passe for currant weight;

Enter Queene.

Madam, you have set all my sorrowes that I ought my freind, vpon my Accompt for my vnworthynes, for soe soveraigne a remedy as your presence;

Queen: Whose distemper is it Moromante, hath detain'd you thus long from the Society? They say you have a freind= =shipp soe neare you, & soe refin'd as you are wounded through it; what paper's that you seeme to be surpriz'd wth, in your hand?

Mor: The tendernes of freindshipp Madam, is the best, constitution of it; & misfortunes that fall vpon our freinds, have not their weight broken by the way, but fall heavyer, as they bring them downe vpon vs; This paper Madam, is a part of that I have acted, p*er*sonating the vnhappy Prince, whose sorrowes I tooke soe truely on me, as they doe excuse this insolence of takeing his p*er*son too, in this Meditation on Saphira's death;

Queene: I pray ye let me see't Moromante, Gemella shew'd me verses of yors th'other day, wch I like't well, they were discreetly passionate;

These:

71)

Mor: These Madam I co͞mend more as they concerne me not somuch; I'le read them to you Madam, in the p*er*son of the Prince, vpon the death of the Princesse of Navarr; [Fol. 38b]

Having allow'd my sorrowes choyce of paine.
They have chosen this; they searching still in vaine
The Cause of this strange dart, & though on earth,

2310 *sorrowes*] [1]*s* heavily inked, perhaps false start wrongly inserted 2327 *th'other*] written as one word 2325 *Saphira*] head of *S* oddly formed, perhaps an apostrophe 2333 [2]*they*] *the* BSl 2334 *dart*] *death* FCos, BSt, BPet, 8°

I finde more reason for't, then for her birth;
Curses are now much more then blessings due,
Yet this doth not seeme strange enough nor new,
Mee thinkes heavens wisdome needed not disburse,
Such treasure, to resume it for a Curse;
But as the Benefactors vse or want,
Doth iustefy resumeing of his graunt,
Soe the recalling her doth but imply
Her want brought heaven vnto necessity;
Soe heaven did re=impropriate this wealth.
Not to impoverish vs but store it selfe;
Thus then my thoughts did me some reason show
Because it did transcend all reason so;
Then carryed vp by this rapture above,
I found that all the Gods had bin in love,
Wth her, soe as their Immortality,
Would have been tedious to them, if to dye
Had byn the way to her; soe to be even
Wth all their loves; she died to goe to Heaven;

Queene: The Cause of your paine ought to cease Moramante, if it depend on the finding of a Cause strange enough for this Lamented death; Did you ever see this Princesse of Navarr?

Mor: Never Madam, nor I thinke the Prince; for sure hee could not possibly arrive in Albion before her death;

Queene: Sure Moramante her marriage was her death vnto the Prince; That breath wch bequeath'd her vnto another was her expiration vnto him;

72 I beleeve

Mor: I beleive Madam, the having made her selfe away must [FOL. 39a] needs have lessned much his devotion to her vertue; Nor doe I beleive that e're he meant to love her, but mov'd by a Religious sence of these hazards of her, wch he was accomptable for, did make this search for expiation, & not expectance of her love;

Queene: Sure Moromante, Love is either Iniurious or iniur'd much

2348 *carryed . . . above*] *Carried by this rapture vp aboue* BSl 2351 *dye*] followed by accidental pen stroke, not punctuation 2361 *another*] very cramped 2366 *her*] *hers* FCos, BSt, BPet, 8° 2368 *&*] head blotted

by mens Complaints; for since my comeing hither, I have heard noe p^{r}tence to a misfortune, but love hath had the imputation of it; Surely you knowe what love truely is; that never heard of it but criminated with sadd effects;

Moro: I shall retract all my Complaints if I be soe happy as to be the first that informes you Madam, what it is; and 'tis soe great a service vnto love it selfe, as it hath but one recompence great enough for my reward; True love Madam, is a spiritt extracted out of the whole Masse of vertue, & twoe hearts soe equall in it, as they are measur'd by one another; they are the vessells wherein it is refin'd & heated, mutually by each others Eyes, and ioyn'd by Pipes as subtile as our thoughts, by wch it runnes soe fast from one into another, as the exchange & the returne, are but one instant; And to confirme my Doctrine, you Madam, by this receipt, may make it when you please;

Queen: The reason then that I have heard, love often call'd a poyson, is, when this spiritt is extended to too high a – Degree of heate;

Mor: If it be drawne from good Ingredients, it cannot rise to an excesse: pure love's a vertue Madam, that hath noe ⌢— extreames, & wilde desires take but Love's name, as rash

blasphemers

73·

[Fol. 39b]

blasphemers doe the Gods by an habituall sinne; It is desire Madam, you have soe often heard call'd Poyson; 'Tis true that is a Minerall, wch if it be not well tempred & p^{r}par'd, is very dangerous, but well disposed, it quickens wth vertue all it mixeth wth;

Queene: Mee thinkes Moromante you conclude there must be a conformity of twoe hearts for love's Composure, [but to] – [endeare it by the difficulty] & soe a single one that gets not another to Ioyne wth it, cannot attaine to loves — p*er*fection;

2376 *informes*] written as *in formes* 2381 *wherein*] cramped 2394 *doe*] *e* not well formed *habituall*] written as *habit uall* 2397 *dangerous*] pen slip at end of *s* gives appearance of colon 2400 *Composure*] ^{2}*o* inked twice, altered from *a* 2400–1 *[but to . . . endeare it by the difficulty]*] by eyeslip, see lines 2405–6

Moro: Loves perfection Madam, is such a blessing as the Gods have not left in the power of one to consum̄ate: but, to endeare it by the difficulty, have ordayn'd it should - - depend on the consent of twoe; This rarity in nature els would prove too cheape if every heart could bee possessed of it: Therefore I conclude that love's p*er*fecc̄on must be such a Compacted vnion of twoe hearts soe close, as there is not somuch as a wish left out betweene them;

Queen: You conclude then Moromante that all love is desire refin'd into the purity of vnion, & I have heard Martiro say, Love's soule was made of the impossibility of vnion: How then can these twoe be reconcil'd?

Mor: I have heard of men immurr'd vpp soe long in darkenes, they began to make a sight out of the habitt of privation of it; And soe dispaire at last, may — thus suppose it selfe a light, wch Custome may delude it wth; And such darke visions Madam, are better wondred at, then disprov'd;

Queene: I confesse Moromante I incline more to your — opinion, as the clearer farr; Martiro's lessons are yet too hard, for soe young a beginner as I, I shall

74 acknowledge

acknowledge my selfe your pupill, as the first I — [FOL. 40a] er'e vnderstood love by: I hope you'le come abroad now; pray give me this paper, least it make you fall into a relapse;

Mor: You are a greater Mistris in Love Madam then you knowe off, for I have not told you halfe of that I — have learn'd of you: The repetition of wch would ease me more, then the remove of all my other greifes;

Exit Queene.

I shall acknowledge you the first that er'e I vnder= =stood love by! How well hath she exprest her ignorance in Love, by speaking thus plainely of it! Thus much but vnderstood by her that said it, were Theame enough: But this was said by chance: fortune is soe confident

2418 *habitt*] *tt* heavily inked, perhaps over indecipherable deletion well formed

2426 *selfe*] heavily inked over paper damage, *s* not

in my oppression, as she dares shew me ioyes in her hand;

Pantamora:

Pant: I wonder Moramante how somuch sorrow did remaine for you, since your afflictions have been parted among vs all; & none hath tane a larger share then I;

Moro: I need not Pantamora, excuse this; since all yor sex is interested more in this losse, then any one of ours, soe as you might glory that she was your owne;

Pant: Why then is your sorrow soe excessive? Mee thinkes I can't allowe any passion to raigne in such a noble heart as yours, but love;

Moro: Suppose I did love Pantamora? would you inferr from thence the iustnes of my greifes, & soe conclude mee vnhappy even by fate?

Noe. Mo:

75

Pant: Noe Moromante, it may be [<—>] I beleive soe of your Omen, as I would share somewhat in the direction of your love towards the successe of it: for I should ⌢ impute your misfortune sooner to your owne fault in Choosing, then to fate; [Fol. 40b]

Mor: Suppose then Pantamora I were to love; how would you direct my Choyce towards the appearance of – successe?

Pant: The attemptingnes of yor spiritt Moromante, is not to be frustrated: but you must know, it is not difficulty should most endeare our vndertakings; if wee may rise by easy vnresisting steps vnto an equall height, it is not the scambling vpp a p^{r}cipice that is to bee —– p^{r}ferr'd;

Mor: I suppose all love's successes equally removed from mee; Therefore would I make a choyce whose eminent ~//~// desperatenes might somewhat comfort mee in the –– disappointment of my wishes; such a vertue as yo^{rs} may challenge a Complacency in all it's wishes: That

2443 *been*] *ee* slightly blotted, poor nib 2455] erasure damage with blotting over, no letters visible 2467 *scambling*] for *scrambling*

insolence in me, were more misfortune, then loves - power reacheth to shame me wth;

Pant: If you could learne to wish as I doe Moromante, you'd finde much ease in the avoyding of a hard - resistance;

Moro: As you doe Pantamora? that's nothing: you are in a Condicōn never to wish, but out of Charity to others;

Pant: If soe, they are all imployed now on you, that your – neerest wishes may end wth the same successe as mine;

Mor: And in retorne of this civility I shall wish noe more successe then I beleive is due to you;

Exit Pant:

76 Came.

Came this by Chance? sure 'tis that each one here's an oracle of love: soe that all that's said is ambiguous; but this even in the fairest sence could not divert me from – Bellessa's ridle; [Fol. 41a]

Enter Genorio:

I congratulate Genorio, your admission here; what thinke you of this place? were I not better to stay here a while then venture backe soe soone into that dangerous ayre, where ffidamira breathes?

Genor: I beleeve Moromante (for soe I now must call you) ⌢ This place hath furnish't you wth such an Antidote, you might venture to seeke out ffidamira, & defye the power of her love; you may then much lesse apprehend the danger of the place, from wch she hath now removed all vertue, your ffathers Court;

Moro: Why is she gone from thence? Didst thou call her Saphira mistrusting my obligation of sorrow great enough for her? or hast thou plagues in store for me, & dost p*ro*duce them thus successively least overcharged, I should breake all in peices?

Geno: Noe Moromante, ffidamira is not dead she is only frighted from your ffathers Court, by her feares of too [< >]⌢ –

2477 *finde*] cross-stroke of *f* heavily inked 2487 *Chance*] *C* touched up 2492 *your*] *you* initially written, *r* rather inadequately joined on 2508] erasure damage, no letters visible

conspicuous a life, to avoyd the guilt of others sinnes rumours & Calumny & guided by her vertue, that was even to a Degree of wildenes, is fled, whether, knowne only to the Gods; your fathers care & search hath p*ro*ved that she is hid from all mortality; his care has beene soe inquisitive.

Moro: Noe I'me confident shee's not dead by this Genorio, I could not thus long have been suspended from the sence of such a Curse: she is not somuch as strayed, for the Gods must needs guide her;

Mee

77

[FOL. 41b]

Geno: Mee thinkes you should not name the Gods, wthout remembrance of the bonds of nature, & of piety you stand ingag'd to them in: to releive your aged father; whose tendernes of all your prayers sinckes vnder the pressure of a greater greife; then your vnhappy absence: The flight of ffidamira his goodnes is such as he feares more the imputation of it to the – forfeite of his promise, then hee feeles all his — present sorrowes;

Moro: I will p^{r}sently ease him Genorio of those feares by writing to him as from ffraunce, to thanke him — for such hono^{rs} meant to ffidamira as did make good his promise by her feares, better then assurance could prove it: I will acquaint him too wth the remove of all those sad occasions wch drew me from him: & will promise him a speedy & ioyfull meeting, which I will p*er*forme too; for at the next election, which approacheth now, I will declare my selfe & soe returne; I must now goe wayte vpon the Queene, for my ⌢— acknowledgm^{t} of the honour of her visitt

Exit

Geno: Oh that I could shutt vp these false lights that dazle thus my faith to ffidamira;

2509 *avoyd*] written as *a voyd* 2511 *knowne*] cramped 2535 *next*] *x* small, poorly formed

He pulls his hatt on his Eyes & stands museing *Gemella enters* vnseene

Gemel: I have found Agenor but wth a looke soe heavy as it weighes downe his Eyes, soe as he hath not seene me; yet it is my darkenes that hath soe benighted him; I will stay yet vnseene, & in the deadest time

78 of his

of his Complaints, this Cloude shall breake & give him all the light, whose want obscures him soe; [FOL. 42a]

Geno: Have not my Eyes attracted poyson strong enough to – stopp this breath before I doe breake out into this foule profession of my tainted faith? or may I thus ⌢ — recover if I can breath it out through these opening pores, before it seizeth on the nobler parts? I will take ffidamira's name & try if that can yet expell't, before it fix; This great Cordiall love, vnlike to others, doth improve his vertue by the Habitt, not remitt it; And to inforce what I have taken inward, Her name & memory, I will thus send after the Infection by the same way it did get in, to trye if this can over take it, & bring it back; I will not goe wthout this sheild before me, & thus arm'd I will goe on & challenge even Bellessa now to satisfy my iniur'd love;

Hee pulls out her *Picture*

And to repare my honour, in this strife:
betweene these two: I'le give the odds of life:

Exit

Gemel: I did not thinke to have found Agenor thus or'ecast, he hath out done me in a disguize; he hath black't over his soule. Oh that I had enlightned him, before ⌜that⌝ I had been thus inlightned by him, I will yet finde ⌢ him out before he meetes Bellessa wth that oddes wch he hath offer'd her: I am soe farr from that vanity, as I would not contest wth her, wth lesse advantage given me, then even Agenor for the Iudge,

Exit

2553 *faith*] corrected, *a* from *o*, *ith* heavily inked, *i* perhaps over *t*

2571 *that*] interlined with caret

Scene: 3·
Queene:

What

79

[Fol. 42b]

Queen: What gentle feare is this, that murmurs thus wthin my thoughts? like breath of ayre that seemes to hold discourse betweene the Leaves: I ne're knew any thing yet soe neare love, as the feare of it; But I must still these noyses of my thoughts, for Innocence soe gentle is wee need not take the paines to blowe it; I must not give my thoughts the liberty to play with love as others doe, in beliefe, as it is an Infant that they can rule it;

Moromante:

Moro: Your Maiesty wilbe pleas'd to pardon this breach of your privacy: 'twas to perfect the cure you began by the acknowledgment of my health to yor Ma^{ty}./

Queen: I receive gladly these acknowledgm^{ts} of your health, but not as they bring me any beleife of Contribution to it;

Moro: To assure you Madam of the vertue of your favour, I must acquaint you wth newes by wch I have beene sett vpon since I saw you, that might have pull'd me downe as lowe as did Saphira's death, as I beleive it will afflict the Prince asmuch: *ffidamira's* flight: whether, vnknowne to all the search the king can – make: but now I am soe chang'd into your Creature, that I have sence of nothing: but what comes to me by yours;

Queen: Why doe you thinke hee wilbe much mov'd with this? can any love resist neglect & long absence & yet master both?

Moro: I doe beleive Madam they are strong enemyes ioyn'd but ag^{t} either of them single love will have the better;

Queen: You see Moromante I contynue your pupill still —

80. therefore

2585 *blowe it*] ~ *of* BSl   2594 *Contribution*] *ution* cramped   2598 *you,*] comma very light, perhaps a pen mark

therefore tell me, whether you would choose ag^{t} you to be neglected in contynuall sight, or lov'd inioyn'd to a perpetuall absence; [Fol. 43a]

Moro: You have almost pos'd your Tutor Madam, there is enough to be said in this controversy, to punish your question wth a tediousnes: I must confesse that I would choose the — obiect, & not the speculation; Neglect doth exclude from that wch wee never had, but banishment doth interdict vs that wch is our owne: & soe becomes the greater Curse;

Queene: You preferr then the lymitted pleasure of one sence ⌒ before the large extent of all imaginations: it seemes that you have chang'd that worthy passion brought you to this place, for some you have found here;

Mor: You were once pleas'd to tell me, my case resembled – much the Prince's: in whose name I dare dispute it, not my owne: Doe you thinke Madam the Prince is bound never to love but ffidamira?

Queene: I yeild the Prince is free by her neglect;

Mor: Why did you couple vs Madam, & not lett vs both loose together?

Queene: I should not [t..ke] tax you neither if you lov'd ne're soe many;

Mor: I doe beleive Madam, I am soe vnhappy, as to bee thus indifferent to you: & yet I thinke if you knew whoe I lov'd, you'd punish me, though you could not blame me for't;

Queene: Pray ye tell me not then, Moromante, I doe not – wish to be vniust;

The difference wch I make betweene you & all the world, will make you disagree, most wth mee, And therefore Il'e forbeare to let you know it;

I would

81.

Queene: I would fall out wth noe body for soe litle as to – satisfy a light curiosity: wherefore I'le enquire noe farther of it; [Fol. 43b]

2613 *inioyn'd*] written as *in ioyn'd* 2615 *enough*] cramped 2618 *doth exclude*] *doth but exclude* FCos, BSt, BPet, 8° 2621 *sence*] pen slip on tail of ^{2}e 2626 *not*] cramped 2628 *ffidamira?*] pen mark resembling long comma under *?* 2632 *[t..ke]* perhaps three indecipherable letters 2640] speech heading *Mor:* or *Moro:* missing

Moro: Give me leave Madam to begg this satisfaction, from you, that you'd be pleas'd to guesse: at it; for I have such a divine beleife of you, that I conclude you cannot be mis= =taken in any thing;

Queene To guesse by your opinion it should be wth Gemella shee makes you such a full returne, at least her Com̄endations promise it;

Mor: 'Tis a strange fate that crosseth me, to be dispis'd where er'e I love! but you have guest as neere as if you had nam'd any other in the whole society, And I nowe dare say Madam, that your knowledge is but thus wrapt vp in Clouds to disguize it; I knowe it by my curse, your being thus insencible;

Queene: I must give over then being your pupill; since you would teach me more then I would learne; In these high points Moromante, I vnderstand you not, I'le bring Martiro to dispute [y] wth you, hee may be your Master, & teach you how to love impossibilityes Hee hath promis'd to prove the reason of it: Il'e shew it you Moromante, that will reconcile you to dispaire;

Moro: You have already shew'd me the impossibility & I ⌒ already find reason enough for loving it, your will;

Queene: You are mistaken Moromante more in the finding of my will, then I easily was in the finding of your love; even my ill will; is not soe found; much lesse that wch you seeme to seeke. *(Exit:)*

Moro: Noe certeinty had byn a Torment great enough for me, noe lesse then a dispayring doubt;

This

82·

[Fol. 44a]

This suspention is a wracke, whose wavering slacknes is the height of Torture; shall I declare my selfe & ioyne the name of Prince to that of Lover? No, I – will trye once more the single strength of Moromante, wch if it bee too weake, I'le call in Prince for my – Auxiliary; *Exit*

2650 *guesse*] [1]*e* inked twice, badly formed 2655 *any other*] *a* and *o* blotted, words barely separated 2669–70 *I . . . found*] *I was in the findinge of your love, even my ill will is not easilie found* BSt, BPet, 8° 2671 *seeme*] *ee* poorly formed, [2]*e* blotted

Scene: 4.
Melidoro: Camæna:

Mel: If my owne ioyes were not sufficient to proclaime my debt to you, Camena, the terrours of these sufferings of wch I am now a Iudge, not a party; might well – endeare this security, you have plac'd me in;

Came: Me thinkes indeede wee twoe are only fixt, the rest in perplexed motions, crosse one another, what a storme of passions are among vs now?

Mel: Wee Camena are arriv'd at loves suppremest Region, – where there is all Cerenity & evenes: & from hence looke on others, that are gott noe higher then the second Region, where there is alwayes roughnes & stormes;

Cam: This is the passage of wch Moromante, Genorio and Martiro are now disputeing, I doe confesse I pitty – – Moromante, & would I could wish mine into Bellessa;

Mel: Why doe you thinke Camena, that Bellessa & Pantamora are not mov'd? doe you thinke women are like windes that doe not feele the stormes they rayse?

Cam: I doe beleive Bellessa's soe vnmov'd she doth not vnder= =stand the stormes you speake of; Pantamora hath a restles humour, to wch no motion is disquiet nor noyse a storme;

Love:

83

Mel: Love can make his approaches according to the heart it sett's vpon: All hearts have outworkes wch must bee taken first, Civility & freedome of discourse, & love once lodg'd there, begins his batteryes; Moromante hath — taken these outworkes, therefore hee may endanger all the rest; [Fol. 44b]

Bellessa: Gamella

Belles: ffeare not Gemella men are not soe subiect to dispaire the least ambiguous word will save them, they will stay themselves even by the finest thred they cann catch, before they'le sincke;

2683 *Camena*] *e* badly formed, resembles *o* 2686 *wee*] final stroke of *w* inked twice *fixt, the*] what is probably an accidental pen stroke partially covers the comma and joins up with *t* 2709 *Gamella*] for *Gemella*

Gentle Camæna asmuch Ioy waite on your wishes as I dare say you wish to mine;

Cam: Your Condition: & person save your servants the paine of wishes:

Genorio looking on Fidam: picture:

Queen: What's that Genorio, wch your eyes fixedly seeme to call your thoughts vpon? Hath it wthdrawne your tongue too, Genorio?

Geno: It was a litle Manuall of Devotion; I was looking on: it was soe long since, I had almost forgott it,

Queen: Let me see't Genorio, I don't thinke but I can shew you as good a one;

Geno: I beleeve that Madam, sure never any contested wth you, for your face, & I Madam yeild wthout shewing

gives it her.

Queen: Now I must aske your pardon Genorio, This is a -- Devotion I yeild to at first sight, wthout examining how much you are addicted to it, Looke heere Gemella

84 here's

here's a face that makes your colour better then — mine, as you can't blush to see it; [Fol. 45a]

Gemel: Me thinkes Madam, I have some where seene a fface that I should knowe this picture by;
I remember now how 'tis, as I past by the Court, I had a Curiosity (hearing ffidamira soe much talked of, the Prince's Mistrisse) to see her, as I perfectly remember Madam, this is her picture;

Geno: 'Tis true Madam, 'tis her that you have taken from me;

Queen: I have but borrow'd Genorio to restore it to you better by asmuch as our admirations can improve it;

Gemel: It would be cruelty Madam, to keepe it, for sure hee is in love wth her;

Genor: As much as I am wth you Gemella: & if you are -- pleas'd wth lookeing on't, as you seeme, you may be pleas'd to keepe it; I shall love it then better then ever;

Queen: Let not our Civility be soe bold wth your Love, ⌢

2720 *Hath*] lower part of *H* heavily inked 2727 *you, for*] comma entangled with *f*, could be second start on *f* *for*] *to* FCos, BSt, BPet, 8° 2741 *borrow'd*] ~ *it* FCos, BSt, BPet, 8°

Genorio, make much of this picture for they say shee's
fled out of all knowledge;

Geno: Soe may be Madam, she is gon to search that lost, wch
she once cast away the Prince, but had I lov'd her n'ere
somuch, she could not take it ill to be left in your
hands;

Gemel: ffidamira's valuation of her faith, above a Crowne ~ -
assures me she deserves respect;

Queen: Here Genorio take your picture, & in your private —
Devotion recant this dissembling;
Here comes Martiro that is soe tender of his, hee's —
affraid the ayre should fowle the Colours;

My love

85

Mart: My love Madam is not materiall but Elementary [FOL. 45b]
fire, whose purity & rarity makes it imperceptible
I have obey'd you Madam in makeing the Impossibility
of the knowledge of it visibly;

Queene: Wee'le all heare it then, since wee cannot see't. *Come.*

Mart: I'le reade them Madam;

I'le aske noe more loves raptures, why
They speake impossibility:
Since Love hath taught me to beleive & prove.
It is the essence of Transcendent Love,
To make even love Corporiall & subsist,
You must allow't a soule that may resist,
Reason & wonder needs must be that soule
ffor nothing else can reason soe controule
If grosse materiall love doe then aspire
Soe high as wonder for a Soule, then higher,
Must that spirituall & sublimate,
That's not extracted out of will but fate,
Desire's it's soule, & higher must imply:
Then wonder needs impossibility:

Queene: Sure Martiro they that could vnderstand your verses,
might knowe your love, th'impossibilityes to me seeme

2760 *of his*] ~ *mistres picture* FCos, BSt, BPet, 8° 2765 *visibly*] *visible* BSl 2766 *heare*] initially written *here*; very small, barely legible *a* inserted 2780 *Desire's*] *Derives* FCos; *Derive* BSt, BPet, 8°

equall; but wee'l send for Moromante to disprove them
it concernes him;
Gemella pray call him,

Gemel: He comes here Madam, & Pantamor wth him:

Queene. I sent for you Moromante to make good my p*ro*mise
that Martiro would prove the height of love reach't
to impossibilityes, & he hath written out his Argument;
I pray

86.

[Fol. 46a]

I pray ye Martiro reade your verses o're againe they
may endure repetition:

He reades them.

Mor: I conceive your meaning Martiro, that since all loves
must have a soule, as high as wonder, some may rise
as high as Impossibility;
I would only aske Martiro whether his love did not
passe first through his sences vpp to his imaginacon?

Mart: Noe Moromante, my love had ne're soe lowe a thought
as hope, I never did expose it to the hazard of a wish:
The nature of it was Angellicall, at first created ⌢
infinite, wthout neede of propagation;

Mor: Miracles Martiro, are not to be alleadged in this case;

Queene: Learne Moromante of Martiro, to [your] assure your love
thus by makeing it impossible:

Mor: I will learne that Madam of none but you;

Gemella whispers to him this

Gemel: Learne of me to hope;

Exeunt

Pantamora:

[<.>]Pant: Vnles I should vnvayle my love my selfe & soe hang
it out to prophanesse, I cannot put a more transparent
cover over it; I have shew'd it through soe cleere a ⌢ –
Tiffany as the least breath of Moromante would have

2784 *equall;*] , light, perhaps a colon 2791 *they*] cramped 2798 *imaginacon?*] head of *?* badly formed, above a comma 2800 *a*] blotted 2803 *Miracles*] *ra* heavily inked, poor nib 2804 *[your]*] deleted with single horizontal line and rough cross 2811] letter erased, causing a small hole, before *Pant:*, which is cramped

blowne't away, & he (me thought) did hold his breath, as if he had been affraid to speake;

Sure:

87

Sure womens Lovers are emblem'd well by Cockatrices eyes, it gives if it be first seene a power over it selfe, wch it getts over another, that it discovers first; [Fol. 46b]

But now that I this truth doe prove,
I soone shall leave off this my love
And love will loose by it farr more then I
Men will finde other wayes to Court me by:

Exit.

Gemella:

The Contemplation of inconstancy hath iustefyed Agenor vnto me, 'thas taken off the fault from him & layd it on nature; I finde all things were made for a -- vicissitude of Change; They say the Heavens are in a restlesse motion, And I'me sure the Earth (wch they say) is fix't, is in contynuall Change, It alters soe as wee should not knowe it were the same, did not wee knowe that it must change; In this generall Earth quake, then how can wee hope for vnmov'd ⌒- constancy in love? It is I then for being constant - among these Changes am vnnaturall; This iniury I'le lay on my disguise, & soe discharge him of it; I finde the Gods soe iustly love the Prince, as I am made a sacrifice to his presage of never being enioyed by man;

King alone wth his sonnes letter.

As dying men whose spiritts having runn their course are soe out of breath, they can scarce carry the soule one stepp further; yet sometimes as she is goinge out of them on her owne way, being refresh'd wth some strong Cordiall, the spiritts rise againe & hold her there; This was my case, my spiritts had scarce somuch

2817 *Lovers*] *loue* BSl; *Loves* FCos, BPet, 8°; not in BSt 2822 *And*] *A* heavily inked 2836 *vnnaturall*] written as *vn naturall*

motion left as panting when they receiv'd this Cordiall;

88 *This*

This soe soveraigne a remedy as it has recovered a [Fol. 47a]
King, whose disease was the being soe; I am already growne better then he that ministred this cure Basilino, by as much as I love ffidamira better then he;

Reades in the letter

I thinke on ffidamira now, only by the sence of your affliction: wch had you forgott, I should once more — thinke of her, to reioyce at your forgetting her, and never more;
Now ffidamira I'me free to thinke of thee, wch to doe fully I will forgett even that wch is too hard to doe my Age: I cannot be soe old I have byn all this while in ⌣⌢– wardshipp to my sonne, he hath till now dispos'd of my love, I am but to day come of yeares; I finde my body & my soule soe reconcil'd, the one offers curiosity, the other strength to satisfy it, in a visitt to the *Shepheards Paradice:* It is but · 3 · or · 4 · dayes Iourney; I will p^{r}sently send for my sonne, & soe transform'd repaire thither;

I'le aske noe more of love, but being thus Kind
But to transforme my body to my mind.

Exit

Finis Actus Quarti

89

[Fol. 47b]

90

The song after the
ffourth Act: [Fol. 48a]

Here love hath met wth such a temper'd heart,
Hee's faine to leave his nature, & vse Art;
To get admittance, wch the soule Denyes.

2848 *This*] ink smudged on catchword   2856 *thinke*] *thin* heavily inked; written as *thin ke*

Arm'd at the Com̄on passage of the Eyes.
Soe he in vertues service puts him selfe,
And soe along by her, gets in by stealth:
Where he a servant still remaines, disguis'd
Knowne, but as he in vertue is compriz'd
You have seene others beames shine soe direct
They seeme by that the lesse heate to reflect,
And you have seene in the appos'd extreame
Love shine wth: out the emission of a beame;
You have seene faith & beauty in the Lists.
And faith some way excus'd as it resists
Nature at last shall leave off her disguise
And soe both cleere, & iustefy all Eyes;

91
[FOL. 48b]

92

Queene: Peace wayte vpon your Soules, wch: seeme t'have byn [FOL. 49a]
Such, as you dyed but for reward, not sin.
Our vertues now even in their best extent.
Are but erected for your Monument;

Morom: Wonder of women on whose chastity.
Heaven hath bestowed such a posterity.
As is a selfe Perpetuation:
wth: out the helpe of propagation:
Wee thus your Children in our youthly taske;
Come here to leave our prayers, & blessings aske;

Marti: Divinest lovers 'bove the praise of breath;
So much you scorn'd to ioyne by lesse then death
By wch omission you so much enioy.
As one another would but seeme a Toy:
Accept this Tribute & our soules inspire
Soe farr toward your example, as desire.

Cam: Rest glorious Couples in that greater blisse

2883 *appos'd*] for *oppos'd* 2902 *seeme*] corrected from *seene* 2905 *Couples*] *Couple* BSl

you went to take, when you did leave vs this:
Be pleas'd your vertues back to vs to send:
Now they have brought you to your Iourneyes end;

Meli: *You that were such your vertues askt not lesse*
Reward of Heaven, then all the world to blesse
Even after you were gone: & did entice:
The Gods to let you make a Paradice:
For mortalls, wch your vertues still implore
That following you, we may yet owe you more;

Gemel: *Illustrious lights of honour & of love*
Wee but your shadowes are that shine above,
Vouchsafe your beames, that wee, (as shadowes doe)
May be admitted too, to follow you;

93

Genorio: *Bless'd soules that Coppied heaven out here soe,* [Fol. 49b]
Together as each other not to knowe:
I finde these markes wch Paradice imply
As gaine of sight & losse of memory.
This scruple now doth only here remaine
That I cannot from wishing yet refraine
If it were meant this heavenly residence.
Should but refine & not extinguish sence:
Let it my grosser spiritts soe refine,
As my vndarkned soule may through them shine.

Pant: *ffaire parralell whose soules soe purely mett*
It seeme that they your bodyes did forgett:
Each being more then all the world, forbore.
(they having one another) to have more,
Soe short of you our imitation stayes,
As wee can hardly reach it wth our prayse.

Exeunt.

Genorio stayes alone.

2909 *not*] *t* heavily inked, altered, perhaps from *e* 2915 *lights*] ascender of *h* heavily inked 2923 *scruple now*] erasure damage beneath *p* and *now*, both very heavily inked; ascender above *p* roughly scratched out, no letters visible under *now* *here*] *ere* heavily inked, [1]*e* a correction 2930 *seeme*] for *seemes* 2931 *forbore*] written as *for bore* 2935 *Exeunt*] [2]*e* heavily inked, altered probably from *s* 2936 *alone.*] could be *alone,*

Geno: Me thinkes I finde my minde on wing: loosed from the sences wch like lyme twiggs held it till now; it is soe light, & soe ascendant now, as if it meant to worke above Martiro's; I am already soe farr towards it, as ye beleife that love is not materiall, nor can it be touch'd or grasp'd, I find it is an Independent ayrienes that both supplyes & fills it selfe, I cannot suppose what I should hope, The Inoffensive purity of this love — imboldens me to shew it to Bellessa, It shalbe soe farr from being sensuall, it shall begg nothing but beleife;

Bellessa.

Queene: Your sadnes *Genorio*, seemes to welcome you as I had neede excuse the Interruption of it

Geno: You are soe farr from interrupting of it Madam, as you bring the Cause along wth you;

94 *Have*

Queene: Have you not yet forgiven my curiosity to see the picture? Are you all of Martiro's minde? [FOL. 50a]

Geno: In what Madam doe you thinke I am of Martiro's minde?

Queen: In keeping your love invisible & therefore *are*;

Geno: I am not of his minde in that: I would shew mine because it is such a wonder, 'twill not els be beleiv'd;

Queen: Will you make loving of ffidamira ⌜A⌝ wonder?

Geno: Yes Madam, that were a greater (after having seene you) then that wch I shall tell you;

Queen: I have only leisure to tell you now Genorio that in revenge of this flattery, I will accuse you of it to your freind — Moromante, whoe lov'd the Prince somuch as he will chide you for it: I am now going to a privacy, I must desire you to leave me;

Geno: I am soe curs'd Madam as even truth seemes dislustred by my telling it; I never com̄itted sinne great enough against another to be equall to this punishment of leaving you;

Exit;

2944 *Inoffensive*] written as *In offensive* 2949 *to welcome you*] *soe welcome to you* BSl 2954 *all*] not in BSl 2956 *are*] possibly (and incorrectly) secretary *ace*, as the scribe's secretary *c* strongly resembles his italic *r*, and he occasionally uses the open italic *e* at the end of words in secretary script; *are* is more likely, however, and the use of italic may be connected with the somewhat arbitrary cutting of the sentence from the version in all other witnesses, in which it reads *are displeas'd that wee sawe soe much as the shadowe of it* 2959 *A*] interlined with caret 2967 *I*] lower loop blotted

Queen: Sure Moromante hath imployed his freind Genorio
to save him the shame of speakeing for him selfe: –
Genorio speakes soe boldly it needs [<⟩⟨>] must be for another
I need not be soe slye of this my thoughtfulnes, They
(since all the vertues they should fixe vpon are heere
obiected to me in Moromante) carry love & honour
(but by humility into a lovely arch) on wch my thoughts
may safely passe on to his person, wch is such, it needs
not humility to recomend it; me thinkes my thoughts
would take the aire a litle to [<⟩⟨⟩⟨ ⟩⟨⟩⟨>] refresh themselves;
That Infant love wch is come to visitt them, would
carry them abroad wth him: they shall goe wth him &
be soe civill as to enterteyne him wth musick as they goe;

she sings

95

She sings: [Fol. 50b]

Presse me noe more kind love, I will confesse
And tell you all, nay rather more then lesse,
Soe you'le assure me when I've told you, then
Not to bring me to witnes it to men:
Though thus you're strong enough to make me speake.
Held by the virgin shame you'l be too weake,
I finde that thus, I may be safely free;
Best by this freedome, I ingag'd may bee,:
I find a glowing heat that turnes red hott,
My heart, but yet it doth not flame a iott:
It doth but yet to such a Colour turne,
It seemes to me rather to blush then burne,
You would perswade me that a flaming light
riseing will change this Colour into white,
I would faine in this whity inference:
Pretend pale guilt or Candid Innocence:
If you will tell me wch wthout deceipt.
I will allow you light, as well as Heat:

I finde a gentle drowsynes flye or'e my sences as if
my thoughts had wearyed them: shee sleepes

2974] erasure damage covered by single flourish 2975 *slye*] *shye* FCos, BSt, BPet, 8° 2976 *fixe*] tail of *x* and *f* very faint 2981 *a litle*] written as *alitle* 2981] erasure damage covered by four flourishes, under the last of which a looped ascender is just visible 3000 *faine . . . inference*] *faine know if this whites inference* FCos, BSt, BPet, 8°

Moromante:

Mor: Was it the rapture that my soule is alwayes in, when it Contemplates the Divine Bellessa, that did p^{r}sent her voyce vnto me there in Heaven? Sure it was.

{ Hee sees her asleepe & stands wondring }

Her soule vseles to her body now is gon to visitt – Heaven, & did salute the Angells wth a song, Lett sleepe noe longer be call'd deaths Image, here is an animation of it: sure all the life that sleepe takes from the rest of the[s] world, hee hath brought hither & lives here

[He goes nearer her] Doth the

96

[FOL. 51a]

Doth the ground move to carry me nearer, then my reverence should keepe me, 'Tis true I finde 'tis this Earthynes about me, that moves me nearer, then my soule durst goe, I am soe neare her now, me thinkes as I am all soule; my body on whose carriage it was brought is now recoyl'd; Therefore my abstracted soule may — fall vpon this hand & doe it reverence; [Hee kisses her hand] My spiritt hath found a body in this touch, & such an one, as it cannot conteyne from venturing to touch againe; [*He kisseth againe*] *Belles: wakes.*

Queen: My sences kept not soe ill watch, as not rise vpp against this attempt; I should be glad to finde some body here to - whome I might impute this insolence wch is soe great, as it almost iustefyes you to me, for not having been the Com̄itter of it: was it not some body that's fledd?

Mor: Noe Madam the Innocent is fledd, & the guilty here stayes, my spiritt that was innocent that fled, for feare of being but suspected, & I remaine all body here expos'd to your displeasure;

Queen: Why this excuse adds still vnto the fault, if your spiritt was innocent it seemes you did it but by chance, and had

3008 *Bellessa*] ^{2}*s* badly formed, heavily inked 3010 *was.*] perhaps *was!*; light diagonal pen stroke above point 3015 *the*] altered from *this*, *i* corrected to *e*, *s* deleted with horizontal stroke 3026 *one,*] comma could be pen mark 3029 *not rise*] *not to rise* BSl 3036 *your*] *r* lightly and distantly joined

noe mind to it when you did it; & I can lesse forgive this prophanation then if t'had been intended;

Mor: Oh Madam you have found soe refin'd a Torture, as it -- reacheth to my soule; wch I call Innocent, for haveing beene soe holily & purely fix'd vpon your hand as i'ts there still & therefore Innocent;

Queen: Now I vnderstand your Crime you shall not have somuch favour as my delivery of the sentence: Gemella shall deliver it to you; till then see me noe more;

Exit.

Genorio:

Mor: What sadnes is this Genorio, that diverts even myne to take notice of it?

Had I

97

[Fol. 51b]

Geno: Had I not already tasted of your Ioyes it could not soe afflict me, that I am not trusted wth such a Ioy of yours, as all the Society beleeves, & I have noe cause to doubt, but your not having told it me;

Mor: Thy curse is soe malignant as it infects thee for being but my freind: I had noe ease left but the beleife that I made thee happy, by this concealem^{t} & now the mistake is come to robb me even of that;

Geno: I shall easily Moromante beleive you as miserable as you would have me, if you can be capable of any, – being belov'd by Bellessa, as they say you are;

Mor: Though I had tendernes enough Genorio to be sensible of thy distrust as thy affliction, yet I have noe sence left for this thy scorne, because 'tis mine; Beleeve me Genorio I am as farr from that, as if I wished to feare it;

Geno: Let it not seeme insolence in me then, in this your affliction S^{r} to professe my selfe happy: for I thinke my selfe soe only, as I hope to transferr it vpon you; If it be S^{r} the memory of ffidamira; that darkens all things els vnto you, the light of my gratitude shall disperse this Cloud presently. Knowe S^{r} I am that subiect into whose hands ffidamira hath deposited her ffaith; & Heaven (to Crowne your meritts) prompts

3051 *myne*] fine calligraphic *y* unique to manuscript, surrounding script scrawled though clear 3057 *Thy*] *The* FCos; *My* BSt, BPet, 8° 3059 *the*] *thy* BSl 3067 *Genorio*] ^{2}*o* inked twice

me to a resignation of this divine Mistris: And that you may have her purely herselfe, wthout the abatem^{t} of inconstancy I will make my selfe soe Criminall vnto her that even her loving me should be one wch she can noe more doe then she can doe ill; Therefore S^{r} at this next Election (wch is now wthin 2 dayes) declare yor selfe; I will waite on you to deliver ffidamira to you & then returne hither (wth your leave) to live in the beleife of such a ⌢ pleasednes in my Condicon as you may thinke you have given me more in acceptacon then you have receiv'd;

98 *'Tis too*

Mor: 'Tis soe hard Genorio to beleive that ffidamira can bee given away, as it had need of such a faith of mine in thee to credit it, But I beleive that thou not only cans't, but wouldst doe soe strange a thing for me, but I will not venture to accept it; Glory in this Genorio, that from the depth of my Deiection thou has't had the power to – rayse me vpp, to ioy that thou shalt have ffidamira, as fully with my wishes, as thine owne; [FOL. 52a]

Gemella:

Gemel: I have a Message to deliver Moromante from Bellessa;

Mor: 'Tis welcome Gemella what so'ere it be;

Gemel: She hath comaunded me to tell you she hath thought – much of your Cryme, and findes it such as nothing suffered but once can be punishment enough for; she hath – – – ordain'd you not only to wish it, but to hope it too, & to see her as often as you will: that vpon the racke of Hope she may dayly Torture you; This sentence she sent me wth, wch I hope I have soe deliver'd, as you vnderstand it;

Exit

Mor: I knowe not whether I doe or noe, me thinkes 'tis some what above my Orbe Humble dispaire; But I will – instantly goe & studdy it before her in submission to - my sentence; Genorio I must leave you. *Exit*

Geno: How iustly am I afflicted by my owne offence, Inconstancy; The Princes Change is fallen out to punish myne; How

3078 *purely*] head of *p* heavily inked 3086] catchword *'Tis too* for *'Tis soe* 3088 *thee*] ²*e* badly formed 3092 *Deiection*] blotted alteration, heavily inked, on *Deie*, letters beneath indecipherable 3094 *as*] false start, perhaps beginning of *t* for *thine* following 3100 *she*] *s* heavily inked, false start 3107 *Humble*] written as *Hum ble*

well doth my Curse suit wth my sinne? my addresse to Gemella for Conveyance of my [<⟩⟨⟩⟨>] passion to Bellessa, when she had afore vndertaken Moromante, My observation hath now assured it me; And I am punish'd (as it were by fate) wth an exclusion from the Princes trust, before he cann knowe a reason for it, but this distrust may warrant the p*ro*fession of my passion to Bellessa, wch I will doe;

I have

99

[Fol. 52b]

Gemella:

Gemel: I have sett the Queene & Moromante together; I beleive betweene them twoe, the execution wilbe gentler then the sentence; I am come my selfe to such a perfect ⌢— knowledge of all men, that I doe neglect them all, I have noe sence soe lowe, as to be moved wth any of theire — Iniuryes; I doe forgive Agenor too, soe all the memory I have now left is of my owne fault that it was ever in the power of man soe to offend me;
I confesse I could wish his repentance, only to expiate that fault of mine, my lookes can never p*er*swade him to it; & for that I must put on this Colours contrary: & like a Ghoast appeare vnto him: his owne guilt will ioyne wth me in the p*er*swasion of it; I am resolv'd to doe it this night as he goes to the Temple, His loving Bellessa must needs susteyne it selfe wth such light and ayrie nourishment that apparitions will soone seeme credible; I'le once more change my disguise: I'me sure it cannot succeed worse wth me, then this hath done,

My face inverting, these two Colours right
Puts Innocence in black & guilt in White.

Exit.

Queene Moromante:

Queen: This is p^{r}sumption Moromante not humility, to be pleas'd wth so severe a sentence; But are you not soe humble as to take more of the sentence on you, then I sent y^{u} Hope?

Mor: You may safely trust my hopeing Madam, Hope seemes soe dull & slow a thing to me, I scarce can thinke it is a

3113] erasure damage with two flourishes covering *when*] cramped 3120 *Moromante*] *M* started twice 3125 *forgive*] *o* blotted 3126 *of*] heavily inked, *f* altered over indecipherable letter 3129 *lookes*] *k* badly formed, ascender inked twice *perswade*] *swa* heavily inked 3133 *loving*] begun *loo*, ²*o* corrected to *v*, *ing* blotted 3143 *humble*] written as *hum ble*

function of the soule: I must have it by infusion not – inherence;

Queene: Sure Moromante it were ill done to give such a meritorious humility as yous, such a Temptation to be perverted as – such a favour;

Moro: It were variety Madam to tell you how much a favour of yours would make me more humble then I am, There could be noe such ill in any body that your wishing but well too,

100 *would*

would not amend, much lesse any vertue that it would not improve; [Fol. 53a]

Queene: You have already Moromante forgott your sentence, the ⌢ - giving of you the Hope to punish you by the frustration of it; Me thinkes since you are soe subiect to forgett your sentence, A favour done you would give me a greater advantage over you; ffor you would quickly forget [<–>] why [<–>] I did it, & enterteine such hopes as would enlarge my power of punishing you;

To himselfe

Moro: It were more Iniury to her to thinke this treachery, then - - insolence to beleive it pitty; Let me suffer Madam on the same place where I comītted the offence;

Queen: A Prince's Eye Moromante, but by a casuall looke, suspends the Execution, but an Admittance to their hand is an – absolution to their Crime;

Mor: That holds not wth me Madam, for your sight was – appointed for my execution; & soe (the rule inverted) your hand must be the higher punishment;

He puts of her glove & kisseth her hand.

Queen: Yours Moromante is soe new a Case to me I knowe not what to say to it: But I had neede imploy my power while I am yet a Queene: It may be that only makes the Defeature of of your hopes a paine to you;

Mor: There are Thousand qualityes in this hand, the least of them above all mortality can name, I consider soe

3150 *yous*] for *yours* 3152 *variety*] *vanity* BSl 3153 *humble*] written as *hum ble* 3158 *the Hope*] blotted, probably poor nib 3161 *why*] blotted, *w* cramped, written over an erasure in an over-long space, paper slightly damaged and brown; no letters visible, gaps on each side filled with a short horizontal stroke 3170 *to their*] *of the* BSl 3172 *inverted*] written as *in verted* 3175 *Yours*] blotted 3178 *had*] blotted 3179–80 *of of*] for *of* 3182 *mortality*] *y* inked twice

litle your quality of Queene as I dare say that's the least p*ro*portion betweene vs; could I beleive you could thinke soe lowe, as to be pleas'd even wth the name of Queene, it may be hope might not p*ro*ve a punishment;

Queen: Why Morom: if I had that desire, could you satisfy it?

Mor: Easier Madam then to be belov'd [by] ⌜of⌝ you, even when I had done it; The conquest of a Kingdome would be easy you being p*ro*pos'd but for Queene;

I could

101

Queen: I could afflict you then Moramante, had I a minde to bee a Queene; but I will not because I have forgiven you; [Fol. 53b]

Exeunt.

Pantamora:

The reason why Moromante see's not Bellessa's love, that's fixt vpon him, must needs be that [.]he lookes vp to high for it; had he but look't, in a naturall & easy levell towards her he must needs have found her very neere him; sure his Eyes were thus stretcht vp into the ayre, when I shewed it soe fayre before him, & he saw it not, but I cannot envy Bellessa in such a Declination as a discending from a – throne, the expectation of wch hath ray'd me above all other thoughts, Bellessa sure will leave the Paradice wth Moromante, The advantage is so sure among all the rest, that it lessens the glory of it; *(Exit.)*

Genorio:

Now am I soe compleatly miserable, I cannot call my affliccon misfortune, I have told Bellessa my fortune soe directly she seemes not to vnderstand it: sure it had too wilde a – – boldnes, it looked liker madnes then love, whither but to my selfe, should I repayre for satisfaccon? since I only am my owne offender, therefore from hence will I devine a happines, that shall defye even fortune the adoration of the not to be epithited Bellessa, & only dispaire shall be

3184 *proportion*] *disproportion* BSl 3186 *Queene,*] comma very faint *punishment*] final minim of *u* barely separated from first of *n*, which was perhaps inserted 3188 *of*] interlined with caret *when*] blotted, poor nib 3189 *conquest*] *q* heavily inked, not well formed 3190 *being*] ascender of *b* very heavily inked 3194 *Pantamora*] *Pan* blotted 3195 *Bellessa's*] ^{2}*e* blotted *love*] *l* heavily inked 3196 *[.]he*] *s* probably deleted 3197 *easy*] letter erased under blotted head of *s* 3200 ^{1}*it*] *my loue* BSl 3202 *ray'd*] for *rays'd* 3207 *affliccon*] cramped 3210 *looked*] *d* heavily inked, probably altered from *s* *to*] *t* blotted 3214 *epithited*] ^{1}*i* smudged, including dot

the reason of it, nay I will not exact lesse of my selfe then the allowing Bellessa to love another, & even p*ro*portion my Ioy in that, to what she shall receive by it; This I am soe resolv'd as I could already even tell it ffidamira;

ffidamira enters like a Ghost,

Though ffortune hath taken me at this advantage; before my resolution had time to fall from my mouth into my – heart, yet thus halfe arm'd I will defend my selfe, nay I will suppose thee an Angell, & conclude thou knowest my thoughts, & yet iustefy them by nameing Bellessa; Thou must needs know her if Angells knowe one another, for she is our delegate here on earth., Tell me then (blessed spiritt) wert thou not sent downe to visit her? to fright me thou could'st not come in such a shape;

I am

102

Ghoast: I am soe happy I cannot thinke my selfe lesse soe, for the improbability of thy being ever soe, wch to remove from thee, I am content to impart to thee all the ~//~ – Angellicallnes I will owne; the prevision of thy misfortunes: to wch thy beleife may prescribe some remedyes: I knowe Bellessa somuch better then thou, as I can tell even what shee shalbe; [Fol. 54a]

She a woman, vnto me shalbe
But still an angell vnto thee
And for thy shame too, Fidamira lives
And is an angell too, as she forgives:

Exit

Geno: Sure the Heavens have conspir'd this miracle; & by an⌢- Angell have been pleas'd to assure me, of the Coniuncture that must be betweene Bellessa & Moromante; I will be an Angell now to Moromante by the delivery of this newes wch is such as even the relation of it over payes all his benefitts, I will seeke him instantly; *(Exit)*

3219 *enters*] [2]*e* blotted *Ghost*] *o* heavily inked 3226 *our*] *your* BSl 3231 *impart*] altered from *import* *thee*] [1]*e* blotted 3236 *me*] *one* BSl 3241 *Heavens*] cross-stroke of *H* blotted

The King following
Fidamira as a Ghoast:

Fidam: In what distresse am I? the king mett mee thus att
the Temple doore; since this habitt cannot deliver me
from him; it shall away, & my tongue deliver me to
him;

King: Stay Fidamira whatsoever thou art Angell or Ghoast,
Am I thus curs'd that even thy spiritt is affraid of me?
But in thy lookes I finde noe other signe,
that thou hast ever died:
But that in Paradice thou dost reside:

Thou cans't not bee a Ghoast, & thus outlooke all
Angells;

I must

103

Fidam: I must reveale my selfe & trust him; or his willfulnes [FOL. 54b]
in following me, must needs discover mee; Besides to
morrow is the day that shall vnridle all our Storyes:
I am resolv'd;
Heaven hath been soe carefull of your Comfort S^r^
as it hath made me my selfe againe;

King: If thou livest ffidamira speake on, for I will beleive
soe, as well as if thou wert an Angell;

Fidam: My flight must be reserv'd for a better opportunity,
But vpon promise you will take noe notice of me,
till I advise you, some strange things I will nowe
deliver;

King: Aske noe other Caution Fidamira but thy beleife
that I cannot disobey thee:

Fidam: You are ingag'd Sr The Prince & Agenor are both
here admitted into the order, vnder the names of –
Moromante & Genorio, To morrow is the new Election
of a Queene, & that light will cleere all, wch is yet
obscure to you; remember your promis'd word my
name's Gemella; *Exit.*

King: Goe Fidamira & doubt not my obedience.

Exit.

3272 *other Caution*] blotted, poor nib

Bellessa:

How finely doe they thinke themselves away that let Love close wth their thoughts, intending to wrestle wth it, but love in that instant that it is let in, falls vnder our wills, & like an Innundation all it findes — portable it rayseth vpp & carryes wth it, This love I learn'd of my Tutour Moromante, & I am yet soe strangely bashfull, as the having my lesson soe — p*er*fect makes me asham'd to repeat it, Gemella assures me I have had a Prince for my Tutor; I am glad of that: for though birth & quality be not the onely foundation

104

foundation to build love vpon: yet it is a faire roofe to cover it; I owe some satisfaccon to Moromante, for all his humble sufferings; & it is enough now my going to loves Cabonett to consult whither I shall tell him yet, or noe; I must resolve; [Fol. 55a]

Bellessa in a wood:

Thither where all things looke soe pleasingly, & soe well pleas'd as you must needs be all in love wth one another; ⌢ whither but vnto you should I repaire for Company, to your pure Innocence as ill can never come soe neere, as to be with= =stood; for in your veynes runnes water & not bloud; My breath is yet soe Innocent it will not blast your tendrest purity: & I will trust you soe as to take Councell of you, in the discovery of my love; you are the fitter because you cannot speake; but you may answere me by instinct, as you seeme to enterteine one another, & not speake;

Eccho: Speake:

Queen: Alas Eccho you are too generally free to be trusted: you ⌢ will answere any body, & what they please; Therefore the Gods when they plac'd you here, to secure the secrecy of solitude, restrain'd your voyce, to answer only to those that first spake to you: & soe disinabled you to tell any thing from

3283 *How*] blot on cross-stroke of *H* 3289 *bashfull*] written as *bash full* 3295 *humble*] written as *hum ble* 3296 *Cabonett*] for *Cabinett* 3307 *instinct*] *insti* heavily corrected, *ti* run together, over mostly indecipherable letters, first letter perhaps *g* 3312 *secure*] *cu* blotted 3313 *only*] *on* blotted 3314–15] accidental pen stroke slants from *th* of *thing* through *pr* of *privacy*

one to another, otherwise I would not trust even this privacy wth this word love:

Eccho: *Word love*

Could I answere at that distance, wch thou dost & not bee seene; I would word my Love; I thinke sure thou couldst not be soe confident, hadst thou not alwayes a Curtaine drawne before thee; But let the vnsuspected spiritt of this place tell me if it allow thee for it's speake & I will yeild to it's Genius; & will resolve what me thinkes it would have me to doe;

Eccho: *Doe.*

Now

105

Queen: Now you have answer'd soe well for him, will you — answere for him to me? Dare you promise mee his — Constancy? [FOL. 55b]

Eccho: *I:*

Queen: If he proves soe our prayers shall interceede for thee vnto the Gods, that this thy service in our loves, may expiate thy former fault; & that thou may'st be restor'd to thy body & thy voyce; But if thou now Prove vaine, or hee inconstant I will come back hither, & wth my curses blast the beauty of this false place: I wilbe soe reveng'd, I will not leave it soe much as solitude, but be alwayes here, & wth my lowd complaints, storme it into a troubled Tumult, And for you Eccho I will wth my reproaches force you to answer somuch, as it shall hoarce that litle voyce is left you; Nay I will search out all the Earths concavityes, & fill them vp soe to choake you quite, There shalbe nothing left you hollow to reside in, but Moromante's Heart that I will leave you for a greater punishment, then death: vpon these termes, if you will stand to your Councell, I am Content;

Eccho: *Content.*

Enter Moromante,

3318] speech heading *Queen:* missing 3322 *place*] ? *plase* *tell*] *t* heavily inked *speake*] for *speaker* 3330 *vnto*] cramped 3333 *But*] with false start, first down-stroke inked twice *now Prove*] clumsy correction on *now P*; *now* cramped and not well formed, down-stroke of *P* very heavily inked with paper damage under, spreading up to blot *u* of *thou* (3332), to which the head of *P* is joined, with some attempt to scratch out the join 3343 *these*] cramped

Mor: Hearing Madam you were gon this way I made hast after you:

Queen: I may now Moromante (in returne of a request you made to me once, to guesse of your love) desire you to doe soe, at the reason of my comeing hither;

Mor: It may be Madam, that love him selfe, in love wth you, – hath given you this curiosity, of rifling his Cabinett, to try who he holds intelligence wth, soe to discover love's secretts, you came hither;

Queene: Hath this Eccho runn vnder grownd & carryed him my voyce [to herselfe]

'Tis true Moromante, to discover love's secretts I came; but more to trust then suspect, & I have found heere

soe

106

soe vninteress'd a Councellor, as he ask'd nothing but words to gratify him, & he hath answer'd me as fitly as if he had sudyed my case before, If you have any suite Moromante speake to him, he is in his Closet here, among these Trees; He is old, & a litle deafe, you must speake loud & he will answere you? [Fol. 56a]

Mor: This is cleere enough I vnderstand it [to himselfe]

You know I have a suit Madam, & I will trye if you have retain'd him ag^{t} me, Tell me then faithfull — Speaker, doth Bellessa Love?

Eccho: *Love:*

Mor: It is to great a miracle to beleive but from any voice but yours; [to her]

Queen: It is my voyce Moromante & I have lett it loose from mee: that it might not have somuch as modesty to hold it back, beleive it, for if you put me to take it into me againe, I have a virgin cold that will not let it speake soe cleere:

[*He kneeles*]

3358 *'Tis*] smudged 3360 *vninteressed*] written as *vn interessed* 3362 *sudyed*] for *studyed*, with perhaps an abandoned attempt at correction: second minim of *u* has been extended upwards with a new pen stroke 3371 *to*] descender of *t* heavily inked *but*] blotted, perhaps false start

Mor: I will beleive it soe as I will worshipp it: All my soules – facultyes shalbe converted into this one beleife, & give me leave to begg for this kinde voyce, that for my sake is soe vnhappy to goe out of you; that you would now take it into you againe: & let me heare it in that Temple: where if it should speake lower my beleife hath eares, to save you the paines of streyning it too high;

Queen: Rise Moromante vnles you had rather wish an answere from Queene then from Bellessa; I have had long a sence well fitted, to your sufferings; & the first thought I did allow your love, was soe civill as it brought me in returne of it, & by this exchange [<–>] stor'd me wth thoughts wch were soe cleere, as they seem'd glasses for vertue to dresse her selfe by not shadowes to draw over her, Therefore I have continued the enterteinm^{t} of your love;

Iudge.

107

[Fol. 56b]

Mor: Iudge Madam how absolutly you are Mistris of my love: It hath held Intelligence wth you, & given & received p^{r}sents from you wthout any knowledge; I will not call this treachery; for I will allow all that is mine to bee yours More: But hath not my love been soe true to you Madam as to p*ro*pose to you it's p*er*fection, in the admittance of my heart into yours?

Queen: It hath propos'd that wch I cannot answer yet, because I know not yet who it speakes to;

Mor: The Heavens conspire a parity in all! (to himselfe) Bellessa give me leave to wish you any thing rather – then an Angell; If you be mortall you can have noe scruple;

Queen: Gemella (although she hath not told me what you are) hath assur'd me you are not what you seeme, & soe an agreem^{t} now would be voyd on both sides: Therefore take this watch wth my p*ro*mise before it measure three howers, you shall knowe me & my story; The times admitts not the telling of yours now; for I must p^{r}epare for the Ceremony of the new Election;

Mor: I will confesse only thus much now Madam, that I am more

3381 *voyce,*] comma very faint 3387 *Queene*] *a* ~ BSl 3390] erasure damaged covered by horizontal stroke 3392 *continued*] with unnecessary minim, not quite complete, between *t* and *i* 3396 *any*] *a* inked twice 3411 *times*] *tyme* BSl

then I doe seeme: even more in love wth you then I can seeme. I accept this pledge of your promise: & will trye;

If time in this despaire doth seeme to move,
slower, or towards the promis'd Ioyes of love;

Exeunt.

Romero:

Rom: Sure nature did make vp our lives in wreaths, & the first instant motion is sett ag^{t} the sence, & soe we move in a continuall revolution to vnwinde our selves, & by the same degrees that wee vnwreath our lives, wee find a slacknes & an enervation in those p*ar*ts that loosen first; our leggs are first vnioynted, soe by degrees this loosenes riseth vpp, & slackens soe the frame of man, as all the p*ar*ts vnfazing, at

108 last

[FOL. 57a]

last seeme but to have a Contiguousnes & noe connection, soe that man is brought by ruine vnto rest: I am soe neere this last dissolving turne, as I will now lay my selfe downe on this soft grownd, that I may fall a peeces wth lesse paine: I have visible misery enough to assure me of pitty. This head on wch the sun it selfe doth snow, & cold cann only thaw it, but my other misfortunes are vnspeakeable; The losse of twoe such Princes in my Charge, as the safety of a Nation depended on; [..e]; Besides another Angell now vanish'd from among vs out of my hands; My Inquiry hath been such (as had she beene vpon Earth) it must needs have mett wth the report of her; should I goe back to the aged King that hath soe soule left but ⌒⌒ expectation? & soe take his soule too away, & then live to see vnfortunate Navarr ly like a headles Trunke, subiect to the first power that would seize it? Nay I will lay my selfe downe here, & by the application of all these horrors to my soule trye if I can fright it out of this weake body;

Genorio:

I have sought Moromante every where but in loves Cabinett

3416 *promise:*] *:* possibly pen marks 3423 *sence*] *scrue* BSl 3425 *slacknes*] *nes* cramped 3428 *vnfazing*] *vnfastning* BSl 3429 *connection*] *e* poorly formed 3432 *soft*] *o* inked twice, perhaps altered from *a* *a peeces*] joined distantly by light stroke 3437 *; [..e];*] first letter of deletion with descender, perhaps *p*; [1] *;* inserted after deletion made, without [2]*;* being deleted 3441 *soe*] *noe* BSl

& cannot find him: sure fortune is scrupulous of letting me have so much Ioy, as the obligeing him, wth such newes as I doe bring him, Here is a stranger, The Gods assist you S^{r} in all your wishes;

Rom: Pardon me if I dare not somuch as wish you well: least fortune, that hath vnder taken the opposition of all my – wishes might by them be brought ag^{t} you;

Geno: Have you ever bin in love S^{r}?

Rom: Never S^{r} I have not knowne soe light a greife, in all my life;

Geno: Comfort your selfe then for you are not soe vnhappy as you might have beene, But I forget my hast S^{r} I must leave you;

Exit.

Stay S^{r}

109

Rom: Stay Sr Hees gone! how strangely is this young man transported wth his passion? but he hath rays'd into me a greater passion, by the sight of a Iewell that he weares: It is the same that Prince Pallante had when he was slaine in the sacke of Pampelona, I wilbe admitted into the society & learne at better leizure, when he got it; [FOL. 57b]

Exit.

Enter Bellessa: Fidamira:
having mutually related their storyes & discover'd themselves to each other;

Queen: What doe women vse to say Gemella in the discovery of their loves?

Gemel: As their severall humours are Madam some thinke all they can say too litle, others speake noe more, then may keepe their lovers from dispayre;

Queen: And I thinke that the safest: for soe wee reserve a — power over our selves, to make them happy & restraine them from making vs miserable by their neglect, but Gemella I am much indebted to you for this discovery

3468 *sacke*] *k* heavily inked 3480 *their*] raised black line through loop of *h* *from*] slight paper damage under *f*
3484 *much*] accidental pen stroke starts *m*

of your selfe & fortune;
Gemel: Could I Madam as easily make you a retribution
of your favours, as I have done of your story,
I should be happy in despight of all my misfortunes,
but I am soe farr from requitall of them, that you
I begg more, your voyce, power & secrecy;
Queen: This ffreedome is a double obligation as it gives me
some meanes of a returne; Doth it not grow late;
Gemel: Looke on your watch Madam I beleive the hower
of Audience drawes neare;

'Tis

110

Queen: 'Tis soe indeed let's goe; [Fol. 58a]

Scene: Last:
Bellessa and all the Society:

Queen: Let the Pretender be call'd in.

Romero lookes amazedly:

You may begin.
Romer: Pardon this amazem^{t} Madam, all my soules facultyes are
drawne into myne Eyes; 'Tis she, it must be she; Nature
ne're made twoe such:

He kneeles.

Blessed Saphira I coniure you by the affliction of your
aged ffather, & the hazard of a Nation answere to this
name, & in one word speake me happyer, then ever the
youngest here can hope to speake;
Geno: The vertue of this place reacheth not here, to the cure
of distraction; you would have Bellessa revive the dead,
hee may be dismiss'd;
Belles: Stay Genorio, sure I owe him more pitty that would -
receive me, then one that would Antedate my death;
worthy Romero, I will answere to that name, & to - -
inlarge this p^{r}sent of my selfe, I will bring a witnes

3494] three diagonal pen strokes through *o* of page number *110* 3501 *Madam*] *M* blotted 3507 *one*] *o* inked twice 3509 *reacheth*] *eth* slightly blotted, poor nib 3513 *receive*] *revive* BSl

thy sonne, whose flight wth me (if it need forgivenes) cannot be denyed now;

Marti: She that hath bless'd you so cannot be denyed yours for me;

Romer: Pardon me Madam if I yet refuse a thought soe lowe as finding of a sonne, you must have all my soule a while, till I have discharg'd my selfe of what I owe yor father, Doe you heare the distresses of your ffather? that cry soe loud in the losse of you, they heare not the

the

III

[Fol. 58b]

the cryes of all his kingdome, for their exposure to the first strange power, that will seize it; His age must - - quickly leave the first invader for his heire, you knowe your brother Prince Pallante perish'd at the seidge of curs'd Pampelona, being an Infant, since the King your father destin'd you to the Prince of Castile, A Prince y^{t} was thought a match to your vertues, as well as Condition, in the time of his treaty you fled, attended only by my sonne; I (vpon whose [< >] trust this misfortune lay like treason) have been ever since in search for you: & now the Gods have beene pleas'd to blesse my ⌒ dispaire: wth what they deny'd me hope, The finding you;

Bellessa: I doe confesse *Romero*, all you have alleadg'd against me, But 'twas not the ease & honour of this place that could divert me from the sence of my fathers affliccons whose releife I did deferr to bring it to the most — entire after the Princes marriage should have - - remoov'd all subiect of dispight, between vs; Heere I resolv'd to stay till then, confident that my ffather would consent to the estimation of my selfe in the expression of an equall vnwillingnes, to that wch his passion to ffidamira did avow;

Romer: This was a sence Madam you ow'd your vertue ⌒ whilest the princes insensiblenes seem'd to provoake

3533] erasure damage, blot *trust*] [1]*t* heavily inked, originally joined to a preceding letter, now erased 3536 *finding*] cramped 3538 *against*] cramped 3541 [2]*to*] *o* blotted 3545 [1]*the*] *t* heavily inked 3547 *avow*] *v* heavily inked, with correction over indecipherable letter

it to a valuation, but the same vertue pleads for his Acquittance now, who hath left ffidamira and taken his course to finde you, seeking your pardon; Therefore Madam in my minde you owe the – King your ffather, this satisfaction for all the sufferings he hath endur'd, a returne of full obedience;

Wee all

112

Society: Wee all ioyne in this supplication for the Prince; [Fol. 59a]

Belles: I wish the King & Prince somuch happines, as it were presumption to beleive I could afford it them. Let me aske you some questions of my ffather:

They whisper.

Gemell: Mee thinkes Moromante you are too cold an interceder for the Prince that seem'd somuch concern'd in all passions;

Mor: Therefore Gemella I may be thought partiall vnto him; your vninterressed prayers Gemella, may challenge more [<~~~~~>] successe; What say you Genorio that can report away, Princes lives soe easily;

Geno<.> Since my fault is an exaltation of your happynes that will aske pardon for it;

Belles: Sure Moromante knowes the Prince best of any body; I will informe my selfe of him: Moromante now you knowe me fully, & my story, give me your advice, I wilbe Councell'd by you in the dis= =poseing of my selfe;

Mor: Confident of all you say Madam, I shall begg of you to pitty the Prince;

Belles: Is your Charity Moromante, somuch above your love?

Mor: It is my love that expresseth nothing but my Charity;

Belles: Well for your sake Moromante, it wilbe easy for me to yeild to asmuch as you shall desire for him;

Mor: I will noe longer seeme to owe you lesse Madam, then I doe;

3553] stroke filling the line joined up with *e* of *the* 3565 *vnto*] cramped 3567] erasure damage covered by four flourishes 3570 *Geno<.>*] *Geno* followed by heavy black mark, raised slightly from the paper, with damage going through to verso; lower point of colon just visible beneath

I doe account this a full pardon; wch is soe strange a one, as it makes me a Prince & the same that you have p*ar*don'd & soe I'le serve this grace; I doe now resigne it back to you:

You

113

[Fol. 59b]

You are already acquainted wth my story; I doe now entirely prostrate my selfe vnto your will, & forgetting all that may direct me to an expectation, I bow my selfe to take [<~>] yor pleasure on me;

Belles: Thus then Moromante, I retract all that I said as – Bellessa, but 'tis to say more as Saphira, & therefore now I confirme my promise of being Councell'd by you in the disposeing of my selfe as farr as my fathers consent shall goe along wth it, wch (I thinke) will not retard our Ioyes,

Moro: Vouchsafe to call me your selfe Madam, soe shall you be Councell'd & obey'd together;

Belles: Moromante hath soe farr p^{r}vayl'd wth me, as I have not only forgiven the Prince: but resolv'd to enterteine such thoughts of him here after, as his afflictions shall p^{r}sent worthy of me;

King: Give me leave then Madam to p^{r}sent the Prince to you: that he may loose noe more time in the⌢- application of himselfe to the desert of your — further pitty; | he pulls of the disguize.

Belles: He hath lost noe time in that S^{r} if he were to begin now, I should not soe soone assure you Sr But I trust you somuch, that if I had one heere to answer for me, as you may for him vpon your twoe words, I should not feare to ingage my selfe;

King: By this it seemes you knowe I am his father, I should much ioy Madam to have that name inlarg'd soe farr as to comprize you;

Belles: You S^{r} that are a father, knowe what I owe to that name: & therefore I beleive you will choose to aske it of him, whose giving it, must iustefy my ioying ⌜in⌝ it:

Now S^{r}

114

3586 *soe I'le serve*] *to deserue* BSl 3590] erasure damage with blotted line over 3617 *in*] interlined with caret

[Fol. 60a]

Now S^r give me leave to retire to the new Election; wee will leave you S^r wth your son; The time cannot stay long;

King: I have forgot to day Madam, that I am King, & if you will have me remember it, it shalbe but to obey you wth the more meritt;

Belles: Let me desire Camena your voyce to follow mine to day; if it seeme to oppose your reason for a while, I p*ro*mise you it shall not doe soe long;

Cam: I resigne my voyce freely to you Madam; *(Exeunt)*

Moro: Now S^r be pleas'd to transferr all my Ioyes wth yor blessing vpon Bassilino;

King: I will not knowe to day soe stale a Ioy as Bassilino, this is thy birth day wherein all is new; & I owe more vnto thy name of Moromante, then thou dost to me for Basilino; I'le have all thy story anon related, I'le tell the now p*ar*t of mine in private;

They whisper

Romer: Give me leave S^r to consider well this Iewell;

Geno: You have bin soe lucky S^r to day in finding what you had lost, as I may feare you'l challenge it;

Romer: If I could challenge it rightly, you should get by it, 'Tis the same are you at somuch leisure to tell me, how you came by it?

Geno: I can direct you how you shall knowe it: aske the King or the — Prince; I knowe nothing of my selfe but what they have told me;

King: I have told you all, wch you must yet conceale;

Mor: Is Gemella ffidamira? & doe you resolve to marry her?

King: I tell you I love her as much as you can Bellessa; Me thinckes – Morom: you seeme troubled at it, Is it that any one should love as much as you?

Mor: It is but the admiration S^r of the strangenes of this day;

Romer: Give me leave S^r I beseech you, to begg somewhat of you in this day, wherein there is noe Ioy but giving;

King: It is noe longer mine, what you desire S^r.

Romer: 'Tis but a true answere to a question;

King. That can't be call'd a guift, I owe it you;

They whisper.

oh:

115

3619 *stay*] *seeme* BSl 3621 *remember*] written as *remem ber* 3622 *seeme*] cramped 3642 *Bellessa*] *sa* inked twice 3646 *somewhat*] *a* heavily inked

Mor: Oh Genorio the king my ffather is in love wth Fidamira, [FOL. 60b]
& is Resolv'd to marry her;
Geno: Mine shall not then be the least Contribution to the wonder
of this day, for yor sake S^r I can resolve never to see her
more, & soe make my happines, the sacrifices of his solemnity;
Romer: Is this certeine S^r that he was sav'd at the sacke of Pampelona?
& this Iewell found about him?
Kinge: 'Tis as certeine as any thing vpon earth, & that my sonne being
then a Child begg'd his life of me, wch he hath ever since lov'd
better then his owne;
Romer: Then (great S^r) it is the Prince Pallante, you have sav'd; I
that was trusted wth him & the governm^t of Pampelona
can assure it; you may remember you surpriz'd the Towne
when I was absent; twoe Princes were then vnder my charge
This & the other daughter Miranda, both Infants, The
generall execution, that was then com̄itted to the rage of
sencelesse multitudes, left vs noe hope of any safety for
these Princes, & now the Ioy of Prince Pallante wilbe soe
great to the good king, that it would exceed beleive, did not
it come from Paradice: good S^r be a witnes to this claime
I shall make,

He goes to Genorio

Now S^r I must not only challenge this Iewell but you too;
Geno: You loose in the value of this Iewell by takeing me wth it,
what plot's this S^r?
Romer: You did remitt me to the king even now for knowledge of
your selfe; you'le not refuse him Creditt;
Therefore be pleas'd to put off that vnhappy name Genorio,
& call your selfe Prince Pallante, sonne to the now blessed
King of Navarr;
Genor: I vnderstand you not S^r
King: Heare him he will teach you what heaven hath destin'd
you, Happy Prince;
Romer: This Iewell I have somuch inquir'd of, is witnes to what
the King hath byn pleas'd to acquaint me wth; Therefore

116 *S^r*

S^r let me begg of you, to owne yo^{r}selfe, & soe at once enlarge [FOL. 61a]

3653 *Resolv'd*] false start with long *s*
Geno, *e* of *Kinge* cramped before colon

3656 *sacrifices of his*] *sacrifize of this* BSl
3663 *governm^t*] head of *g* heavily inked

3659 *Kinge*] heavily written over

your selfe, wth power of an acquittance to this brave Prince;

Geno: The Improvemt of my life must be the same still of my – – obligation to you Sr

Moro: Have you this blessing too, to give that my ffathers haveing ffidamira, shall prove your wishes;

Geno: I have now only left that Devotion, you had for the Princesse of Navarr, for expiation of my fault;

Mor: Conceale this purpose for a while, you may chance finde her where I found Saphira;

Geno: This Change of my fortune if it prove happy Romero to me: it will assure me of a Recompence of thy fidelity;

Rom: I have not a wish left, but the finding of the Princesse Miranda too, & the miracles of this day make nothing desperate;

Pantamora hastily running:

Pant: Heaven hath sent you hither opportunely Sr to defend the rights of this Society, The will of the ffoundresse (wch appoints the Queene to be chosen principally for her beauty, is now violated in Gemella, who now is chosen / En: Bell: all the Ladyes.

King Is she chosen Queene as a Moore?

Pant: Vnles heaven hath wrought a miracle for her since she was so, when she was chosen;

King Could you forget Iustice Madam? you are too much interested in gratitude to Beauty, to be consenting to this choyce;

Belles: I should be vniust to beauty Sr should I disavow it; Thus I iustefy my choyce, expecting admiration, not exception; [she pulls off her scarfe.]

Gemel: None can wonder somuch as I Madam that you would expose yor selfe to the blemish of an errour for my sake;

Belles: What say you Ladyes now to this choyce;

Cam: 'Tis such a one as hath asmuch Beauty as your leaving of the place admitts of;

Nature.

117
[Fol. 61b]

Gemel: Nature carryes me to pay this Duty: [to Bonoso.]

Bon: I dare owne this Ioy though scarce the honour of this day; This place is soe fruitfull in miracles to day

3692 *wishes*] *wishe* BSl 3704 *beauty,*] for *beauty)* 3708 *heaven*] *v* heavily inked 3714 *not*] *noe* BSl
3720 *Nature*] long vertical pen stroke under, and joining, *e* *Bonoso*] always *Bonorio* in other witnesses

as there hath been one in your absence Madam, wch is noe wayes a lesse miracle then yours: but as it is a blessing sent to you, wch abates the wonder of it;

Moram: leads *Geno*: towards *Bellessa*

Mor: 'Tis soe strange a thing Madam as wee may bragg we have a p^{r}sent worthy of you: A brother, this Prince Pallante;

Belles: I am so forward as I will not stay to be mov'd by reason, but on the wings of your faith will fly to imbrace Pallante as my brother;

Pallante: Sure Nature Madam, saw her defects in me, & meant to cast me away: & made you Madam soe corrected a p*er*fection, as you cannot be beleiv'd to be of the same hand;

Belles: I will answer all yor Complem^{ts} Pallante by calling you brother: & soe returne halfe back vpon your selfe;

Geno: I have a suit now, wch I deserve soe litle, as I must ioyne you two in an intercession for me to the Queene, I will not somuch vndeserve her p*ar*don, as to desire her love;

Belles: Were your fault greater then my Creditt wth her, her owne vertue would assure yor p*ar*don;

Geno: 'Tis more I p*er*ceive then you knowe Madam, I pray ye lend me this vayle not to cover it, but to reveale it: for it is soe black a fault, as the passing through this colour will lighten it:
Let this Fidamira wch was a Cover to your Innocence, prove one vnto my guilt;

Fidam: I have soe long agoe forgiven you it, that I had almost forgotten it: Therefore S^{r} put of this the only marke for my memory;

Belles: Can you tell *Morom*: (I cannot choose but call you soe still) my brothers fault to Fidamira:

I beleeve

118

[Fol. 62a]

Moro: I beleive I can Madam;

Bell: I pray you tell me then, I long to knowe it:

They whisper.

As Fidam: talkes wth the King Romero lookes on a Iewell of hers, & a watch on her Arme

3728 *as*] blotted 3733 *defects*] ascender of *d* heavily inked 3759 *watch*] *marke* FCos; not in BSt, BPet, 8°

then goes to Bonoso her father
& talkes wth him;

King: Now Fidamira 'tis time for me to Challenge the reward of my obedience: wch I thinke soe meritorious, as it shall aske noe lesse then your selfe for a Recompence; my Ioyes are yet to come, & I am happy only in the power of dis= =pensing wth the Election;

ffidam: Oh Sr 'tis not in my power to satisfy you; I have made a vow of Chastity: wch is now out of my power to recall;

King: What strange crosses doth my passion meete wth, first it was to contest wth nature, & now wth heaven;

goes sadly
away.

Bellessa having whispred wth *Moram:*
speakes to Pallante;

Belles: If I had knowne this story of you Pallante, I should not soe easily have own'd you for my brother: but 'tis forgiven now;

Geno: If I had knowne you sooner for my sister Madam, I should not have needed this forgivenes;

Romer: Will you be pleas'd to heare me summe vp now all the — ioyes of this day? This Fidamira ⌜is⌝ the Princes Miranda, This Gent: (her supposed father) hath (by my knowledge of this Iewell & a marke vpon her arme) confess'd to me, that he sav'd her life, at the same time, when the Prince sav'd Pallante: & to avoyd the rigour pronounc'd against such disobedience, he own'd her for his Child, & soe hath bred her ever since;

This

119

Bon: This Sr my Conscience (vpon Romero's Challenge) bids me avow; [Fol. 62b]

Mor: There was but this one point wanting to close vpp all the blessings of the circle of this world;

Belles: Lovely miracle, sure heaven did deferr the knowledge of you; till the acquaintance wth your vertues, should make the finding you a sister, such a ioy as now it proves;

Fidam: Matchles Saphira, I cannot now tax nature for any of my wants since she may answere me; that she reserv'd them all for you;

3775 *now*] cramped 3778 *summe*] final minim of ^{2}*m* blotted 3779 *is*] interlined with caret 3784 *his*] *s* heavily inked, badly formed, a correction over an indecipherable letter *bred*] cramped 3793 *wants*] cramped

King: Nature & Heaven ioyning now, have master'd my passion: ⌒ Miranda, I must aske you pardon; & since your vow hath -- chosen this residence; I will p*ro*pose to the Society, the con= =firming of you Queene, during life;

All: Wee all agree to it with Ioy;

Fidam: I accept this as an Accomplishm^{t} of yor p^{r}diction Moram: of my never being enioy'd by man; & now heaven inspire me with a prævision of your happines, wch I dare assure;

Bellessa's love wch you doe now possesse:
May by you only, be made more, or lesse;

Mor: I will leave her only the power of improving it; And I will be incapable of lessening it;

Belles: I have now a suit to you S^{r} soe great, that I must ioyne Moromante in it; 'Tis to obteine leave for my brother, to be receiv'd a suitor to the Princesse Arabella, yor Daughter: whose Beauty fame p*ro*miseth asmuch, as birth assureth for her vertue;

King: This day is somuch auspicious, as all my owne wishes are offred me; I p*ro*mise you Madam she wilbe ready for his acceptance, or refusall;

Geno: This rayseth the value of my new Condition, the p*ro*curem^{t} of such an honour as the Princesse Arabella: whose lustre adds Beauty to the Crowne, not that to her;

Mor: I have one suit to you more S^{r} that you would be pleas'd to give me leave to keepe this happy name *Morom:*

120 *You*

King: You may in gratitude qualify'[.] that name, y^{t} hath serv'd you soe: [FOL. 63a]

Belles: I will keepe Bellessa to all my life;
What say you Camena & Melidoro? you twoe are tun'd for your part in the Consort of this day;

Cam: I am soe transported wth your ioyes, as I have quite forgott my selfe;

Melid: Give me leave then to remember you of your p*ro*mise to my wish if Belles: left the Society wth Moram:

Belles: All is due Camena, that was p*ro*mis'd on that Condition;

Cam: Then Melidoro you are M^{r} of your wishes;

Belles: Wee will carry you to Court wth vs, where wee wilbe witnesses of your Ioyes; you see Pantamora, every one that durst scarce hope their wishes, possess'd of them to day: & yor security is only left empty;

3819 *Morom*] *M* heavily inked 3819] *o* corrected in catchword *You* 3820 *qualify'[.]*] letter erased, blotted, possibly *s*

Pant: I shall stay here Madam, & learne to bound my wishes wthin the peace of this blessed place;

Bell: Come Martiro, I thinke of nothing now, but the makeing thee happy too: wch is soe hard, it will require my study;

Marti: That is easily done Madam, by leaving me here: my prayers you shall have alwaies, in stead of me;

Mor: Will you be pleas'd Madam, to thinke who we shall dispatch to yor father, wth this newes; & to demaund his consent to the Prince Pallante's wish & mine;

Romer: Let me begg this Com̄ission, that I may imploy this new life you have given me, in yor service;

King: None can be soe fitt as Romero that can informe the King of all that's past;

Bon: Give me leave Madam to make the last suit to be receiv'd into the Society wthout a publication of a p^{r}tence;

Fidam: 'Tis a Grace S^{r} you may be assur'd of, since it is in my power; Amongst all these Ioyes it is no wonder if noe body thinke of sleepeing; Let vs retyre Madam to that rest wch may prepare vs for to morrowes Ceremonyes.

Marti: It behooves me Madam to have the last wish;

May

121

[Fol. 63b]

May you have all the ioyes of Innocence
Enioying too all the delights of sence:
May you live long, & knowe all, 'till y'are told
(To endeare your beautyes wonder) you are old;
And when Heavens heate shall draw you to the skye:
May you transfigur'd not disfigur'd dye:

Finis.

122.

3833 *peace*] blotted 3836 *Marti:*] *rti* clumsily written, *r* perhaps altered 3847 *Fidam:*] blot on head of *F* 3850 *morrowes*] cramped 3851 *Ceremonyes*] ^{1}*e* not well formed 3855 *all*] *not* FCos (interlined), BPet, 8°; not in BSt 3858 *dye*] altered from *lye*